INVENTORY OF THE HERPETOFAUNA AT
HOPEWELL FURNACE NATIONAL HISTORIC SITE

Harry M. Tiebout III

Technical Report NPS/PHSO/NRTR-03/089

Department of Biology
West Chester University
West Chester, PA 19383

June 2003

Cooperative Agreement
4000-9-9016
Amendment 1

National Park Service
Northeast Region
Natural Resource Stewardship and Science
200 Chestnut Street
Philadelphia, PA 19106-2878

Table of Contents

List of Figures

List of Tables

Summary

An inventory of amphibians and reptiles at Hopewell Furnace National Historic Site (HOFU) was conducted from July 2000 through November 2001. Two methods were used: general herpetological collecting and anura calling surveys. These methods were used to inventory the herpetofauna in 14 habitat types: upland forest, lowland forest, weedy fields, pastures, animal pens, hay fields, corn fields, open wetlands, vernal pools, runs (small streams), French Creek, rock fields, buildings and associated grounds, and mixed habitats (consisting of two or more of the above). These 14 habitat types encompassed virtually the entire park. For all habitat types combined, 33 surveys were conducted, averaging 6.5 person-hours per survey.

Twenty-five species were encountered at HOFU, including eight salamander species, six frog species, five turtle species, and six snake species. These represented 45% of the 55 species potentially occurring in the park, as estimated from previous reports and published range maps, and included eight new records for the park: longtail salamander (*Eurycea l. longicauda*), northern dusky salamander (*Desmognathus f. fuscus*), northern red salamander (*Pseudotriton r. ruber*), eastern milk snake (*Lampropeltis t. triangulum*), northern black racer (*Coluber c. constrictor*), red-eared slider (*Trachemys scripta elegans*), common musk turtle (*Sternotherus odoratus*), and wood turtle (*Clemmys insculpta*). Of the 560 individual encounters for all taxa, the most common species was the red-backed salamander (*Plethodon cinereus*), which comprised 40.9% of all encounters. The next three most abundant species were the northern two-lined (*Eurycea bislineata*, 17.7% of encounters), northern dusky (13.0%), and four-toed salamander (*Hemidactylium scutatum*, 3.8%).

On average, a given species was found in 2.8 of the 14 habitat types, with a range of from one to seven habitat types used per species. The common garter snake (*Thamnophis s. sirtalis*) and wood frog (*Rana sylvatica*) were found in the most varied habitats, being found in seven and six habitat types, respectively. Thirteen species were found in only two or fewer habitat types, and six species were found in only a single habitat type: longtail salamander, northern red salamander, black rat snake (*Elaphe o. obsoleta*), eastern milk snake, northern ringneck snake (*Diadophis punctatus edwardsii*), and common snapping turtle (*Chelydra s. serpentina*). The most species-rich habitat type was upland forest, supporting 14 of the 25 species (56%). Three other habitat types were nearly as species-rich: runs (11 species), lowland forest (10 species) and French Creek (eight species). Collectively, these four habitat types contained 23 out of the 25 species (92%). The two species not found in these four habitat types, longtail salamander and eastern milk snake, were both found only in and around buildings.

Species that were not detected by the inventory were categorized as "probable current residents" if they had been previously documented in the park, or if HOFU fell within their geographic distribution and the park appeared to contain enough suitable habitat. Six such species were identified: eastern newt (*Notophthalmus v. viridescens*), northern leopard frog (*Rana pipiens*), northern brown snake (*Storeria d. dekayi*), northern copperhead (*Agkistrodon contortrix mokasen*), eastern painted turtle (*Chrysemys p. picta*), and spotted turtle (*Clemmys guttata*). Additional inventory surveys are recommended to confirm the status of these species.

The following species were identified as potential indicators of ecological health for the four most species-rich habitat types: red-backed salamander (upland and lowland forest), four-toed salamander (lowland forest), northern dusky and northern two-lined salamanders (runs), and northern green frog (*Rana clamitans melanota*) and pickerel frog (*Rana palustris*, both for French Creek). In addition, four taxa were identified as species of special concern for HOFU and therefore in need of special management: four-toed salamander, spotted salamander (*Ambystoma maculatum*), red-eared slider, and wood turtle. Two habitats were found to be of special concern for HOFU and hence in need of further management. Areas designated as potential bog turtle (*Clemmys muhlenbergii*) habitat warrant a comprehensive survey for this species by a certified surveyor, and the vernal pools should be monitored following the protocols in the Amphibian Research and Monitoring Initiative of the United States Geological Survey.

Acknowledgments

Funding for this project was provided by the National Park Service (NPS) and West Chester University (WCU). The following NPS personnel are thanked for their contributions: S. Ambrose, C. Almerico, E. Clark, J. Collins, F. Hebblethwaite, G. Martin, and R. Ross. Many WCU students and community volunteers assisted in all aspects of the project. Of these, D. Koronkiewicz, and M. Myers are especially thanked.

Introduction

Status of Natural Resource Data Sets in 2000

As reported in the most recent resource management plan (RMP; for definitions for this and other acronyms and terms, see the Appendix) for HOFU (updated in 1999), eight of 12 basic natural resource data sets the park needs had begun, and one was currently on-going. For the biological resources, species lists had begun for some taxa (e.g., reptiles and amphibians, Yahner et al. 1999), the mapping of vegetation had begun (Russell 1987; Vanderwerff 1994), but as yet species distribution maps had not been started. T. W. Bowersox and D. S. Larrick (PSU) had studied the requirements for conducting a long-term monitoring program of vegetation in the forested ecosystems of HOFU (Bowersox and Larrick 1999). In addition, park staff had been monitoring white-tailed deer three times annually using herd counts, and they had established deer study plots and exclosures in 1992 to monitor impacts of deer on forest regeneration; although neither of these activities has been pursued since 1996. Richard Yahner and colleagues had recently begun a bird inventory. However, as of 2000 there had been no systematic inventories completed of wildlife in the park.

In the HOFU RMP, Project Statement HOFU-N-602.002 (Title: Inventory & Monitor Faunal Resources) calls specifically for the "accurate assessment of all animal species." To meet this objective with respect to the herpetofauna of HOFU, the following project goals were developed.

Project Goals

Based on discussions with John Karish, Beth Johnson, and Ed Clark (beginning 18 November 1999) and two scoping workshops held at HOFU (6 July 2000 and 25 January 2001), the following park-specific objectives were developed. First, an inventory was to be designed and implemented to determine presence/absence for each species in each of 14 habitat types surveyed during the inventory. The intention was to obtain the most complete list of species possible for the entire park, not to conduct a quantitative comparison among habitat types. Second, these data were to be evaluated to determine if (a) any of the major habitat types support species that could serve as future indicator species for the ecological health of that habitat type, and (b) any species or habitats are of special concern to HOFU and warrant additional study (to be funded and implemented as a separate project) or management.

Methods

Study Area

Hopewell Furnace National Historic Site (HOFU) is located approximately 10 km northwest of Pottstown, PA, on the border of Berks and Chester counties. HOFU encompasses 343 ha (848 acres) and is situated in the Piedmont Upland Section and the Conestoga Valley Section of the Piedmont Province (Genoways and Brenner 1985).

According to Russell (1987), the park is dominated (75%) by forested habitat composed primarily of oaks (*Quercus* spp.), ash (*Fraxinus* spp.), elm (*Ulmus* spp.), tulip poplar (*Liriodendron tulipifera*), red maple (*Acer rubrum*), and black walnut (*Juglans nigra*). Red cedar (*Juniperus virginiana*) occurs only in the early successional stands. Approximately 17% of the park consists of agricultural areas, maintained as row crops, hayfields, and pastures. The remaining 8% of the park includes developed areas and historic sites. The entire park is drained by French Creek and its tributaries. In addition, according to Delaware Valley Orienteering Association Maps, HOFU contains some vernal pools near the Visitor Center, and several wetland areas are scattered along the creeks and throughout some of the lower-elevation sections of forest (Delaware Valley Orienteering Association 1992, 1999). HOFU ranges in elevation from approximately 280 m in the extreme northeast corner to approximately 140 m where French Creek flows out of the park. The park is bounded on the west, north and east by French Creek State Park, on the south by State Game Land 43, and on the southeast by private farm and forested land.

Predicted Species List

Several protocols for inventorying the herpetofauna and other terrestrial vertebrate species have been tested at HOFU (Yahner et al. 1999). As part of these studies, the authors compiled numerous sources of existing information on the herpetofauna of HOFU. The predicted species list (Table 1) for the current inventory is based on Yahner et al. (1999), Tiebout 2003 (from nearby Valley Forge National Historical Park [VAFO]), the now-obsolete NPFauna database, and the NPSpecies database as of 21 July 2000. Table 1 includes the sources of information for each species, the Integrated Taxonomic Information System Taxonomic Serial Number, and legal status (state and federal) for each species.

During the course of the inventory, additional information became available on the geographic distribution of many of the predicted species (Hulse et al. 2001) and on the availability of habitat needed to support individuals of certain species. Accordingly, at the completion of the inventory, the predicted species list was revised to incorporate this new information (see "Revised Predicted Species List and Future Inventory Needs" below).

Sampling Design

Based on vegetation maps (Russell 1987; Vanderwerff 1994), orienteering ground cover maps (Delaware Valley Orienteering Association 1992, 1999), three site visits made prior to the inventory, and new habitat types encountered during the inventory, a total of 14 habitat types were identified and surveyed (Table 2). The most extensive terrestrial habitats and French Creek are mapped in Figure 1. French Creek was considered a distinct habitat type (i.e., different from

Table 1. Predicted list of amphibian and reptile species at Hopewell Furnace National Historic Site.

Group	Common Name	Scientific Name	ITIS TSN[1]	Predicted List - VAFO[2]	Predicted List - HOFU[3]	HOFU Occurrence Status[4]	HOFU NPFauna Database[5]	Official Species[6]	Legal Status[7]
Salamanders									
	Eastern (Red-spotted) Newt	Notophthalmus v. viridescens	173616	X	X	PTC		NPS	
	Eastern Hellbender	Cryptobranchus a. alleganiensis	208175		X	R			
	Four-toed Salamander	Hemidactylium scutatum	173678	X	X	PTC			
	Jefferson Salamander	Ambystoma jeffersonianum	173598	X	X	R		NPS	
	Longtail Salamander	Eurycea l. longicauda	208310	X	X	R			
	Marbled Salamander	Ambystoma opacum	173591	X	X	R			
	Mountain Dusky Salamander	Desmognathus ochrophaeus	173641	X	X	R			
	Northern Dusky Salamander	Desmognathus f. fuscus	173634	X	X	R			
	Northern Red Salamander	Pseudotriton r. ruber	173681	X	X	R			
	Northern Spring Salamander	Gyrinophilus p. porphyriticus	208355	X	X	R			
	Northern Two-lined Salamander	Eurycea bislineata	173685	X	X	PTC		NPS	
	Red-backed Salamander	Plethodon cinereus	173649	X	X	PTC, PO	X	NPS	
	Slimy Salamander	Plethodon glutinosus	173650	X	X	PTC		NPS	
	Spotted Salamander	Ambystoma maculatum	173590	X	X	PTC, PO	X	NPS	
	Valley and Ridge Salamander	Plethodon hoffmani	173657		X	R		NPS	
Toads & Frogs									
	Bullfrog	Rana catesbeiana	173441	X	X	R			
	Eastern American Toad	Bufo a. americanus	173474	X	X	PTC, PO	X	NPS	
	Eastern Gray Treefrog	Hyla versicolor	173503	X	X	PTC		Y	
	Eastern Spadefoot Toad	Scaphiopus h. holbrooki	173427	X	X	R			
	Fowler's Toad	Bufo woodhousii	173478	X	X	R			
	Northern Cricket Frog	Acris c. crepitans	173521	X	X	R			
	Northern Green Frog	Rana clamitans melanota	173439	X	X	PTC, PO	X	NPS	
	Northern Leopard Frog	Rana pipiens	173443	X	X	PTC		NPS	
	Northern Spring Peeper	Pseudacris c. crucifer	207304	X	X	PTC, PO	X	NPS	
	Pickerel Frog	Rana palustris	173435	X	X	PTC, PO	X	Y	
	Upland Chorus Frog	Pseudacris triseriata feriarum	173527	X	X	R			
	Wood Frog	Rana sylvatica	173440	X	X	PTC, PO		NPS	

Table 1 (continued). Predicted list of amphibian and reptile species at Hopewell Furnace National Historic Site.

Group	Common Name	Scientific Name	ITIS TSN[1]	Predicted List - VAFO[2]	Predicted List - HOFU[3]	HOFU Occurrence Status[4]	HOFU NPFauna Database[5]	Official Species[6]	Legal Status[7]
Lizards									
	Five-lined Skink	Eumeces fasciatus	173959					Y	
	Northern Fence Lizard	Sceloporus undulatus hyacinthinus	173866	X	X	R			
Snakes									
	Black Rat Snake	Elaphe o. obsoleta	174178	X	X	PO			
	Common Garter Snake	Thamnophis s. sirtalis	174137	X	X	PTC, PO, WOC	X	NPS	
	Eastern Earth Snake	Virginia v. valeriae	174152	X	X	R			
	Eastern Hognose Snake	Heterodon platyrhinos	563935	X	X	R			
	Eastern Milk Snake	Lampropeltis t. triangulum	209242	X	X	R			
	Eastern Ribbon Snake	Thamnophis s. sauritus	174135	X	X	R			
	Eastern Worm Snake	Carphophis a. amoenus	174162	X	X	R			
	Northern Black Racer	Coluber c. constrictor	174170	X	X	R			
	Northern Brown Snake	Storeria d. dekayi	174130	X	X	R			
	Northern Copperhead	Agkistrodon contortrix mokasen	174297	X	X	R			
	Northern Redbelly Snake	Storeria o. occipitomaculata	174132	X	X	R			
	Northern Ringneck Snake	Diadophis punctatus edwardsii	209171	X	X	PTC		NPS	
	Northern Water Snake	Nerodia s. sipedon	174253	X	X	PTC, PO	X	Y	
	Queen Snake	Regina septemvittata	174125	X	X	R			
	Rough Green Snake	Opheodrys aestivus	174172	X	X	R			PT
	Smooth Green Snake	Liochlorophis vernalis	563910	X	X	R			
	Timber Rattlesnake	Crotalus horridus	174306	X	X	R			PC

Table 1 (continued). Predicted list of amphibian and reptile species at Hopewell Furnace National Historic Site.

Group	Common Name	Scientific Name	ITIS TSN[1]	Predicted List - VAFO[2]	Predicted List - HOFU[3]	HOFU Occurrence Status[4]	HOFU NPFauna Database[5]	Official Species[6]	Legal Status[7]
Turtles									
Bog Turtle	Clemmys muhlenbergii	173773	X	X	R			FT, PE
Common Musk Turtle	Sternotherus odoratus	173758	X	X	R			
Common Snapping Turtle	Chelydra s. serpentina	173753	X	X	PO, WOC	X	NPS	
Eastern Box Turtle	Terrapene c. carolina	173777	X	X	PO	X	NPS	
Eastern Painted Turtle	Chrysemys p. picta	173784	X	X	PO		Y	
Red-bellied Turtle	Pseudemys rubiventris	173814	X	X	R			
Red-eared Slider	Trachemys scripta elegans	173823	X					
Spotted Turtle	Clemmys guttata	173771	X	X	PO		Y	PT
Wood Turtle	Clemmys insculpta	173772	X	X	R			

(1) Integrated Taxonomic Information System - Taxonomic Serial Number (from http://www.itis.usda.gov/)

(2) Predicted species list for Valley Forge National Historical Park (VAFO) reported in Tiebout (2003).

(3) Predicted species list for Hopewell Furnace National Historic Site (HOFU) reported in Yahner et al. (1999).

(4) Occurrence status for provisional list for Hopewell Furnace National Historic Site (HOFU) reported in Yahner et al. (1999).

    PTC = Observation while conducting a protocol
    PO = Personal observation
    WOC = NPS wildlife observation card
    R = Predicted occurrence from published range maps

(5) Listed on the NPFauna database (http://endeavor.des.ucdavis.edu/nps/park.asp?park=CHSOHOFUO)

(6) NPS = in NPSpecies Park-Species List as of 7-21-2000
    Y = reported by Yahner et al. (1999) but not in NPSpecies as of 7-21-2000

(7) FT = Federally Threatened, PC = PA Candidate, PE = PA Endangered, PT = PA Threatened
    as reported in Wild Resource Conservation Fund (1995)

Table 2. Description of 14 habitat types inventoried for herpetofauna at Hopewell Furnace National Historic Site.

Habitat Type	Code in Database	Additional Description
Upland Forest	UF	deciduous forest not subject to flooding, does not have standing water
Lowland Forest	LF	deciduous forest in floodplain of French Creek or of lower Baptism Creek, level terrain with standing water or subject to seasonal flooding
Weedy Field	WF	uncultivated fields, usually the power line right-of-way
Pasture	PA	grassy fields for grazing of domestic stock
Animal Pen	PEN	fenced area for holding sheep, other stock
Hay Field	HF	cultivated hayfields, mowed regularly
Corn Field	CF	cultivated corn fields
Open Wetland	OWET	wetlands with little or no canopy, may be seasonally wet only
Vernal Pool	VER	any of several vernal pools located in the southern floodplain of French Creek between Hopewell Lake and Hopewell Village
Run	RU	within 1 m of small streams, includes all runs, Baptism Creek, all tributaries to Baptism Creek, all tributaries to French Creek
French Creek	CRK	within 1 m of French Creek
Rocks	RCK	areas of large rocks or boulders, with or without forest canopy
Building/grounds	BLD	historical structures, residences, park buildings, and associated grounds
Mixed Habitats	MIX	mixture of two or more habitat types

Figure 1. Map of three major habitat types at Hopewell Furnace National Historic Site (upland forest, lowland forest, and French Creek), plus the locations of fields. The fields include pasture, hay fields, and corn fields and are numbered sequentially following a convention used by the natural resource managers.

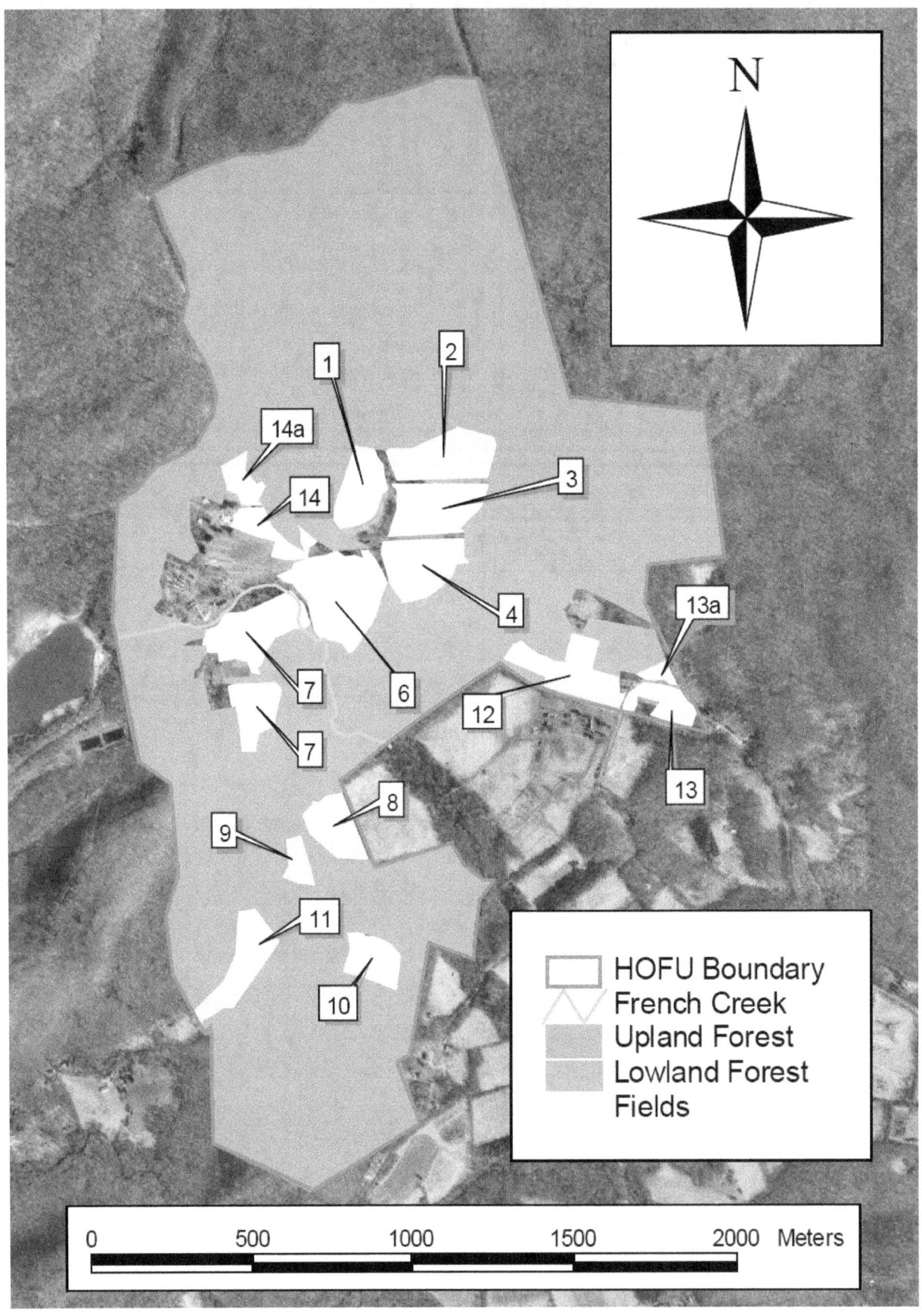

the other lotic systems) because it had considerably greater discharge rate, came from a unique water source (piped from the bottom of Hopewell Lake), and was the only lotic system to flow through agricultural land. Virtually the entire park was surveyed, with the exception of employee residences, historical structures, and most park buildings and their associated grounds.

Survey Methods

Two survey methods were used, general herpetological collecting and anura calling surveys, as described below. These methods were chosen for their efficacy, relatively low cost, and ease of use (Campbell and Christman 1982; Simons 1995; Yahner et al. 1995, 1999; Seigel and Doody 1996; Tiebout 2003).

General Herpetological Collecting (GHC)

Seigel and Doody (1996) found GHC to be the best method for generating inventory species lists, accounting for 71% of the total reptiles found, 89% of the total amphibians found, and detecting 47/50 (94%) of the total herpetofauna species at one of their study sites. GHC typically consists of (a) traveling an area on foot to observe animals that are above ground and visible, (b) turning and replacing natural and artificial cover objects, (c) searching in and around burrows, crevices, hollow logs and other refugia, (d) nighttime road-surveys, (e) seining and dip netting small bodies of water, and (f) visual scanning surveys (using binoculars and spotting scopes) of aquatic habitats to identify basking animals. GHC is not constrained to standardized times or transects, but instead relies upon the past experiences and professional judgment of the investigator. Because of this, GHC is not intended to be a quantifiable or replicatable survey method. Instead, it is used to detect the most possible species. In the current inventory, GHC was used in two different ways. Opportunistic GHC was conducted in conjunction with anura calling surveys (see next section), and included all other species that were encountered as surveyors moved about the park listening for frogs and toads. Planned GHC was conducted as a scheduled survey to search particular areas of the park for animals. When all or part of a planned GHC survey targeted just one or two taxa, it was considered a taxon-specific planned GHC survey. These taxon-specific surveys were used in a special effort to detect species that were on the predicted list but were not being detected by the regular planned GHC. Examples of taxon-specific survey methods that were used include: (a) black rat snake - visually scan woodpecker holes and other cavities in standing snags during early morning basking hours, (b) mole salamanders (*Ambystoma* spp.) - conduct night surveys of small, isolated woodland pools in early spring to detect breeding adults, (c) bog turtle - probe soft submerged substrate with poles in appropriate habitat, (d) northern copperhead - search south-facing, open rocky slopes potentially used as basking, denning, and birthing sites, and (e) queen snake (*Regina septemvittata*) - search along streams with abundant rocky substrate and overhanging vegetation during cool, sunny mornings.

All of the planned GHC conducted on a given day was considered a single survey. A given survey typically covered a number of different habitat types and regions of the park. A total of 29 GHC surveys were conducted between 6 July 6 2000 and 25 November 2001. On average, each GHC survey took 6.9 person-hours to conduct (see Table 3 for GHC dates and times).

Table 3. Dates, methods, numbers, times, and total person-hours spent for each of the 33 surveys conducted during the herpetofauna inventory of Hopewell Furnace National Historic Site.

Survey Date	Survey Method [1]	Survey Number [2]	Time Begin [3]	Time End [3]	Total Person-Hours [4]
07/06/00	GHC	1	12:00	16:00	4.00
07/07/00	GHC	2	10:30	16:30	6.00
04/29/01	GHC	3	10:15	15:45	13.33
05/06/01	GHC	4	10:00	14:30	4.50
05/15/01	GHC	5	9:10	16:00	6.25
05/23/01	GHC	6	16:00	19:00	3.00
05/28/01	GHC	7	11:15	16:15	4.00
07/26/01	GHC	8	9:50	15:17	5.45
07/27/01	GHC	9	9:30	13:40	4.17
08/14/01	GHC	10	9:25	13:51	4.43
09/13/01	GHC	11	9:45	18:01	20.22
09/19/01	GHC	12	9:30	17:00	15.00
09/21/01	GHC	13	9:20	15:45	12.50
10/30/01	GHC	14	9:30	15:30	13.00
10/10/01	GHC	15	9:15	15:15	12.00
10/11/01	GHC	16	11:25	14:40	3.25
10/17/01	GHC	17	9:15	15:10	11.83
10/18/01	GHC	18	11:24	14:43	3.32
10/20/01	GHC	19	10:45	15:20	4.58
10/21/01	GHC	20	10:00	14:30	4.50
10/24/01	GHC	21	9:15	15:15	12.00
10/25/01	GHC	22	11:18	16:20	10.07
10/28/01	GHC	23	9:00	12:00	6.00
10/31/01	GHC	24	9:15	12:15	6.00
11/01/01	GHC	25	9:50	14:12	4.37
11/03/01	GHC	26	9:45	14:30	3.75
11/04/01	GHC	27	9:55	11:45	1.83
11/10/01	GHC	28	10:25	11:25	1.00
11/25/01	GHC	29	10:10	11:00	0.83
03/08/01	ACS	1	18:33	19:18	0.97
03/20/01	ACS	2	18:50	20:52	2.75
05/23/01	ACS	3	20:53	22:22	7.10
06/22/01	ACS	4	21:10	22:25	2.77

(1) GHC = general herpetological collecting; ACS = anura calling survey.

(2) Surveys are numbered sequentially for each method separately.

(3) Times are for searching phase of survey only, do not include recording weather.

(4) Total person-hours includes time to conduct survey and record weather data, summed for all participants.

Anura (frog and toad) Calling Surveys (ACS)

Suitable breeding areas were located during the early spring 2001 so that calling surveys could be started at the first snow melt. Five ACS sites were established to serve as listening posts for these potential breeding areas (Figure 2). These sites were surveyed four times (see Table 3 for ACS dates and times) during the spring and early summer, so as to cover the full range of breeding seasons for this amphibian group. On average, each ACS took 3.4 person-hours to conduct. In accordance with the protocols for the Vermont Calling Frog Survey, as recommended by the North American Amphibian Monitoring Program (NAAMP, Mertz 1999), these survey dates were chosen in an effort to include the first spring evenings in which maximum daytime air temperatures exceeded 7.2 °C (45°F), 12.8 °C (55°F), and 21.1 °C (70°F). Each ACS began 30 minutes after sunset, and at each site, observers listened for 3-5 minutes. Observers were able to detect calling anurans within a radius of approximately 300 m. Calls were identified to species, and abundance scored for each species (Table 4, Mertz 1999). This method has the potential to detect any of the frogs and toads on the predicted list.

Weather Variables

Each time a survey was conducted, the following data were collected: (a) Weather Bureau Sky Codes (0-8, see Table 5, Mertz 1999), (b) Beaufort Wind Scale (0-5, see Table 6, Mertz 1999), (c) air temperature in the shade at 2 meters above ground, and (d) relative humidity in the shade at 2 m above ground. Because weather conditions could change over the course of a survey, if it lasted more than 1 hr, these data were collected again at the end of a survey.

Herpetofauna Encounters

The location of each animal encountered was mapped in the field on aerial photographs (digital ortho quarter quads) or on orienteering maps (Delaware Valley Orienteering Association 1992, 1999) and later digitized in ArcView 3.2a. For each encounter, the following data were recorded: species, body length (snout-vent-length, or carapace length for turtles, in cm), gender (if externally identifiable), color morph (for red-backed salamanders [*Plethodon cinereus*] only), and habitat type.

Habitat Use Analyses

Habitat use for each species was assessed in two ways. First, the number of different habitat types used was calculated. Second, a Habitat Diversity Index (HDI) was calculated using the Shannon Index (Brower et al. 1998):

$$\text{Habitat Diversity Index (HDI)} = H' = -\sum \text{Log}_{10}(p_i) * (p_i)$$

where p_i = the proportion of total sightings for a given species that occurred in habitat type i

13

Figure 2. Map of the five anura calling survey (ACS) sites at Hopewell Furnace National Historic Site. Observers at each site could detect calling anurans within a radius of approximately 300 m.

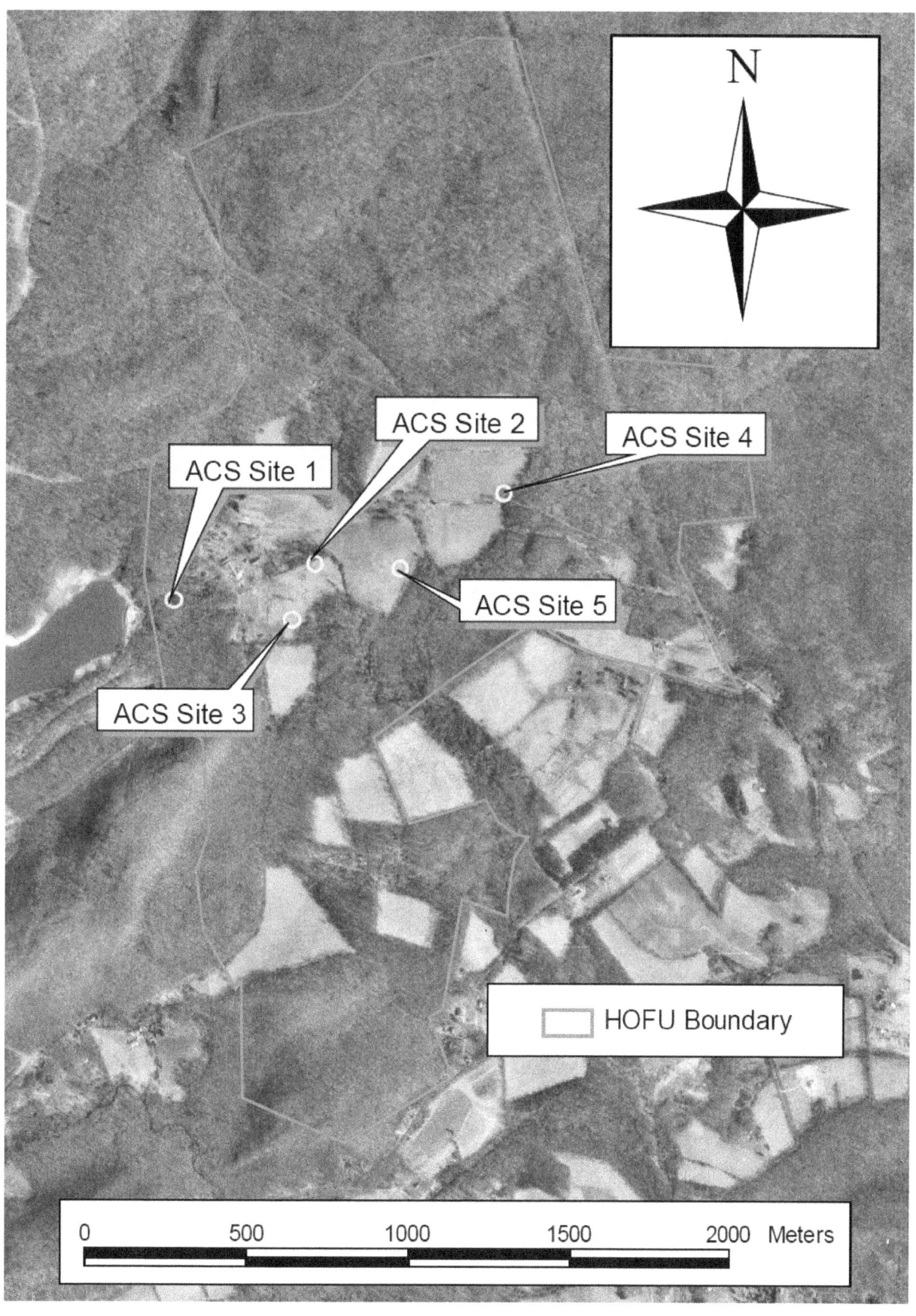

Table 4. Wisconsin Index Values, used for scoring the abundance of calling anurans during anura calling surveys (Mertz 1999).

Index Value 0	No amphibians calling.
Index Value 1	Individuals can be counted. There is space between calls.
Index Value 2	Calls of individuals can be distinguished but there is some overlapping of calls.
Index Value 3	Full chorus. Calls are constant, continuous, and overlapping.

Table 5. Weather Bureau Sky Codes (Mertz 1999), used for scoring sky conditions for each survey.

0	Few clouds
1	Partly cloudy (scattered) or variable sky
2	Cloudy (broken) or overcast
4	Fog or smoke
5	Drizzle
7	Snow
8	Showers

Table 6. Beaufort Wind Scale Codes (from Mertz 1999), used for scoring wind intensity for each survey

Beaufort Wind Scale	Wind Speed km/h	Description
0	<1.6	Calm; smoke rises vertically
1	1.6-4.8	Light air; rising smoke drifts; weather vane inactive
2	6.4-11.3	Light breeze; leaves rustle, can feel wind on face
3	12.9-19.3	Gentle breeze; leaves and twigs move around, small flags extend
4	20.1-30.0	Moderate breeze; moves thin branches, raises loose paper
5	30.6-38.6	Fresh breeze; trees sway

The HDI integrates both the number of different habitat types used by a given species and the equitability of use. Thus, the highest diversity index would occur for a species that used multiple habitat types without being overly dependent on just one or two.

Status of Predicted Species Not Found

Each predicted species not found by the inventory was assigned to one of four residency status categories based on two or more of the following criteria.

Probable Current Resident = this species likely occurs in the park but was not documented during the current inventory.

> Criteria: HOFU is within the current geographic range, HOFU has previous record(s) of this species in the park, HOFU contains suitable habitat to support this species

Possible Extirpated Resident = this species likely inhabited HOFU historically, but has been locally extirpated.

> Criteria: HOFU is within the current or historic geographic range, HOFU has no previous records, HOFU contains some suitable habitat, or possible mechanism for extirpation has been identified.

Indeterminate = cannot determine if species ever inhabited HOFU or whether species likely currently occurs in park.

> Criteria: HOFU may or may not be in current geographic range, HOFU has no previous records, or HOFU contains some suitable habitat.

Probable Nonresident = evidence suggests species does not occur in park, perhaps never occurred in park.

> Criteria: HOFU may be outside of current geographic distribution, HOFU has no previous records, or HOFU contains little or no appropriate habitat.

Species Detected

A total of 33 general herpetological collecting and anura calling surveys was conducted at HOFU, averaging 6.5 person-hours per survey, for a total 214.8 person-hours spent surveying the park. The surveys detected eight salamander species, six frog species, five turtle species, and six snake species, for a total of 25 amphibian and reptile species found during the seventeen-month study (Table 7). The surveys detected none of the two species of lizards that was on the predicted species list (Table 1). All of the species detected were on the predicted species list.

Individual animals were counted for all of the taxonomic groups, except for the anurans (frogs and toads) detected during nocturnal calling surveys. These were scored based on chorus intensity (Table 4). Each time an anuran species was recorded as calling at an anura calling survey site during a survey, it was recorded as one individual. Thus, the anuran encounter frequencies underestimate actual abundance. The maximum chorus intensity recorded for each anura species at each site is given in Table 8.

The most frequently encountered species was the red-backed salamander, which accounted for 40.9% of the 560 encounters for all species combined. The next three most abundant species were also salamanders, including the northern two-lined (17.7% of encounters), northern dusky (13.0%), and four-toed (3.8%). Thus, in terms of abundance, salamanders constitute a major component of the herpetofauna at HOFU (75.4% of all encounters).

Several species appeared to be uncommon in the park, being detected infrequently in this inventory. Species encountered fewer than five times include the wood turtle, red-eared slider, common snapping turtle, eastern milk snake, black rat snake, eastern gray treefrog (*Hyla versicolor*), and longtail salamander.

Habitat Use by Species

Herpetofauna species varied widely in the number of different habitat types in which each was found (Table 7). On average, a given species was found in 2.8 of the 14 habitat types, with a range of one to seven. The common garter snake and wood frog were found in the largest variety of habitats, being found in seven and six habitat types, respectively. Other species found in considerably more habitat types than average included the pickerel frog (five habitat types) and northern two-lined salamander, red-backed salamander, and northern black racer (four habitat types each).

In contrast, more species were found in fewer than the average number of habitat types. Seven species were found in two habitat types, and six species were found in only one habitat type (longtail salamander, northern red salamander, black rat snake, eastern milk snake, northern ringneck snake, and common snapping turtle). All of these latter species were relatively uncommon, falling below the median frequency of encounter.

The 25 species also varied widely in their patterns of habitat use, as quantified with the Habitat Diversity Index (HDI; Table 7). The HDI values were strongly positively correlated with the number of habitat types used per species ($R = 0.88$, $P < 0.0001$ for linear correlation; $R = 0.92$,

Table 7. Encounter frequencies of amphibian and reptile species found at Hopewell Furnace National Historic Site, categorized by habitat type. For each habitat type, the total number of encounters and total number of species are presented at the bottom of the column. For each species, the total number of encounters, total number of habitat types used, and Habitat Diversity Index are presented at the end of the row.

Group	Common Name	Upland Forest	Lowland Forest	Weedy Field	Pasture	Animal Pen	Hay Field	Corn Field	Open Wetland	Vernal Pool	Run	French Creek	Rocks	Building/Grounds	Mixed Habitats	Total No. Encounters	Total No. Habitat Types	Habitat Diversity Index
Salamanders																		
	Four-toed Salamander		14								7					21	2	0.28
	Longtail Salamander													4		4	1	0.00
	Northern Dusky Salamander	1									72					73	2	0.03
	Northern Red Salamander										7					7	1	0.00
	Northern Two-lined Salamander	3	5								90			1		99	4	0.17
	Red-backed Salamander	88	49	3							89					229	4	0.49
	Slimy Salamander	3									2					5	2	0.29
	Spotted Salamander	3	1							1						5	3	0.41
Toads & Frogs																		
	Eastern American Toad	5						1							2	8	3	0.39
	Eastern Gray Treefrog		2												1	3	2	0.28
	Northern Green Frog		1								1	5				7	3	0.35
	Northern Spring Peeper		2						1						3	6	3	0.44
	Pickerel Frog	1					1	1			4	6				13	5	0.57
	Wood Frog	5	2	1				1	1		3					13	6	0.69
Snakes																		
	Black Rat Snake	1														1	1	0.00
	Common Garter Snake	7	3	1							2	5	1	1		20	7	0.73
	Eastern Milk Snake													1		1	1	0.00
	Northern Black Racer	4		2	3									1		10	4	0.56
	Northern Ringneck Snake	5														5	1	0.00
	Northern Water Snake	1							1		2	4				8	4	0.53
Turtles																		
	Common Musk Turtle											4		1		5	2	0.22
	Common Snapping Turtle											1				1	1	0.00
	Eastern Box Turtle	6	1			3										10	3	0.39
	Red-eared Slider					1						1				2	2	0.30
	Wood Turtle								2			2				4	2	0.30
	Total No. Encounters	133	80	7	3	2	3	3	5	1	279	28	2	8	6	560		
	Total No. Species	14	10	4	1	2	1	3	4	1	11	8	2	5	3	25		

Table 8. Maximum chorus code[1] recorded for each species at each sampling site during Anura Calling Surveys at HOFU.

Species	Anura Calling Survey Site				
	Site 1	Site 2	Site 3	Site 4	Site 5
Eastern American Toad		1		1	
Eastern Gray Treefrog				2	
Northern Spring Peeper	1	1	3	1	1
Pickerel Frog	1				
Wood Frog					1

(1) Wisconsin Index Values, used for scoring the abundance of calling anurans during anura calling surveys (Mertz 1999):

Index Value 0	No amphibians calling.
Index Value 1	Individuals can be counted. There is space between calls.
Index Value 2	Calls of individuals can be distinguished but there is some overlapping of calls.
Index Value 3	Full chorus. Calls are constant, continuous, and overlapping.

P < 0.0001 for $\log_{10}$-transformed correlation). Accordingly, the two species using the highest number of habitat types also had the highest HDI values, and all six of the species limited to a single habitat type had the lowest possible HDI value. However, two species had much lower HDI values than would be expected based on the number of habitat types they were found in, a result of low equitability of occurrence among habitat types. The northern dusky salamander was found in two habitat types (upland forest and runs), but exhibited a 99% preference for the latter. Similarly, the northern two-lined salamander used four different habitat types, but was found in runs for 91% of encounters.

Species Richness by Habitat Type

Because sampling effort was not uniform across all 14 habitat types, statistical analysis of the number of different species found in each habitat type could not be performed. Nevertheless, it is possible to gain some qualitative insight into the relative value of each habitat type for the herpetofauna (Table 7). The single most species-rich habitat type was upland forest, supporting 14 of the 25 species (56%) found at HOFU. Three other habitat types were nearly as species-rich: runs (11 species), lowland forest (10 species) and French Creek (eight species). Collectively, these four habitat types contained 23 out of the 25 species (92%). The two species not found in any of these four habitat types, longtail salamander and eastern milk snake, were both found only in and around historical buildings.

Species Detected

This study was successful in making significant additions to the HOFU herpetofauna species list. Eight of the 25 species detected represent new records for the park: longtail salamander, northern dusky salamander, northern red salamander, eastern milk snake, northern black racer, red-eared slider, common musk turtle, and wood turtle. This study detected 25 species out of a possible 55 species on the original predicted list (Table 1), or about 45% of the potential species.

Four-toed Salamander (*Hemidactylium scutatum*)

This secretive habitat-specialist (Shaffer 1991) was encountered 21 times, being found in lowland forest (67% of encounters) and along runs (33%) that flowed through lowland forest. All encounters were in the part of HOFU bounded by Hopewell Road on the north, PA Route 345 on the northwest, and Harrison Lloyd Road on the west. This area contains an abundance of the preferred habitat for this species, described as woodland pools with sphagnum moss (Shaffer 1991). Four-toed salamanders were not encountered in other parts of HOFU that also appeared to be suitable habitat, most notably the lowland forest on the northwest side of PA Route 345. Although there are no recent published records of this salamander from Chester or Berks Counties, HOFU is well within the geographic range for this species (Hulse et al. 2001). In addition, Yahner et al. (1999) detected this species in their recent study at HOFU.

Longtail Salamander (*Eurycea longicauda longicauda*)

This salamander was found only four times during the inventory. All encounters occurred in the Spring House, where at least three different individuals were encountered on the floor under various storage containers. In Pennsylvania, longtail salamanders are known to occur throughout the entire Commonwealth, where they are found in a variety of terrestrial habitats (Hulse et al. 2001). However, during dry periods they tend to move closer to streams and ponds (Hulse et al. 2001). This species is primarily nocturnal, spending days under various cover objects, including bark, logs, rocks, and debris (Hulse et al. 2001). It is likely, therefore, that this species also occurs in some of the natural habitats in HOFU, especially along the many runs and along the more rocky sections of French Creek, even though extensive surveys of these sites failed to detect this species. This species was not detected by Yahner et al. (1999) and represents a new record for HOFU.

Northern Dusky Salamander (*Desmognathus fuscus fuscus*)

This aquatic salamander was encountered 73 times. It was always associated with flowing water, being found in or along runs throughout the park (99% of encounters) and under a foundation stone of an old spring (1%). Duskys were not encountered along the larger French Creek or around the vernal pools in the floodplain of the creek. These observations are consistent with the known ecology of this species, which is wide-spread throughout the state of Pennsylvania, preferring small woodland streams with abundant cover objects (Hulse et al. 2001). This species was not detected by Yahner et al. (1999), and it represents a new record for HOFU.

Northern Red Salamander (*Pseudotriton ruber ruber*)

This salamander was found seven times, always in runs. Most encounters (71%) occurred in runs on either side of PA Route 345, in an area approximately 100-250 m south of the intersection with Park Road. Another encounter occurred approximately 250 m north of the northeast corner of field 2, and a single encounter occurred about 200 m northeast of the northeastern corner of field 10. These observations support the general findings that this state-wide inhabitant prefers cool, clear streams that are shallow and offer abundant rocks on the bottom (Hulse et al. 2001). This species was not detected by Yahner et al. (1999) and represents a new record for HOFU.

Northern Two-lined Salamander (*Eurycea bislineata*)

This salamander was the second most frequently encountered species in the park, with 99 encounters. It was found primarily along runs ((91% of encounters), but also in lowland forest (5%), upland forest (3%), and once (1%) in the maintenance yard. This species was found throughout the smaller lotic systems in HOFU but was not found along French Creek. These observations on habitat preference are consistent with published reports. As summarized in Hulse et al. (2001), this common species, with a state-wide range, is known for preferring small and medium-sized streams with gravel or sand substrates. This salamander was also detected at HOFU during the Yahner et al. (1999) study.

Red-backed Salamander (*Plethodon cinereus*)

A ubiquitous and ecologically important amphibian (Burton and Likens 1975), the red-backed salamander was encountered 229 times throughout most of the park. Most often encountered along runs and in upland forest (38% of encounters each) and in lowland forest (21%), this species also rarely occurred in a weedy field in a power line right-of-way (1%). These habitat preferences are consistent with the known ecology of this well-studied state-wide salamander (Hulse et al. 2001). Petranka (1998) describes the habitat for this species as limited to leaf litter in forested areas, but Hulse et al. (2001) report that in Pennsylvania red-backs are known to inhabit disturbed areas at the borders of forests, such as railroad rights-of-way. Yahner et al. (1999) also found this salamander at HOFU.

Slimy Salamander (*Plethodon glutinosus*)

This secretive, terrestrial salamander (Hulse et al. 2001) was found five times. It occupied upland forest (60% of encounters) and areas along runs (40%) in forested areas. These observations are consistent with other reports, which state that this species typically is found in densely forested areas, especially where there are abundant rocks and logs (summarized in Hulse et al. 2001). However, because this species is solitary and often nocturnal, its numbers are often underestimated (Hulse et al. 2001). In addition, this species may have one of the shortest activity seasons of all salamanders, rarely encountered before May or after mid-October (Pfingsten and Downs 1989), making it even more difficult to detect. Hence, it is likely that this species occurs in additional forested locations at HOFU. Yahner et al. (1999) detected this salamander during their study at the park.

Spotted Salamander (*Ambystoma maculatum*)

This salamander was found five times. It was most often found in terrestrial environments, occurring in both upland forest (60% of encounters) and lowland forest (20%). One individual (20%) was found during the breeding season (20 March 2001) in a vernal pool, where several spotted salamander egg masses also were found. These habitat types are consistent with the known preferences of this state-wide species, which inhabits deciduous and mixed hardwood-coniferous forests that have vernal pools or permanent ponds (Hulse et al. 2001). This salamander was also detected by Yahner et al. (1999), and the range of snout-vent lengths (SVLs, 2.5-9.0 cm) coupled with the presence of egg masses found during the current inventory indicate that HOFU supports a breeding population of this species.

Eastern American Toad (*Bufo americanus*)

Note (for this and the following frog species): The anura calling surveys sampled an area with a radius of approximately 300 m (see "Sampling Design" above). Thus, habitat descriptions based on these data reflect conditions nearest the observers and might not accurately represent the exact habitat occupied by calling anurans.

This terrestrial anuran was encountered eight times during the inventory. During GHC, it was found five times in upland forest (62% of encounters) and once in a corn field (12%). It was also detected twice during ACS, calling at the lowest chorus intensity code from a mixed habitat type (25%). These observations are consistent with the known distribution of this state-wide habitat generalist, which is found in a wide range of terrestrial habitats from open meadows to dense forests (Hulse et al. 2001). Although not one of the most common species at HOFU, these toads were found throughout the park, ranging in elevation from the French Creek floodplain (approx. 146 m) to near the summit of Chestnut Hill (approx. 250 m). This species was also detected by Yahner et al. (1999), and the detection of calling adults in the current inventory suggests a breeding population is present at HOFU.

Eastern Gray Treefrog (*Hyla versicolor*)

This uncommon treefrog was detected only three times during the inventory, being heard calling twice during GHC and once during ACS. All detections were made at ACS site 4 in lowland forest or mixed habitat types. These encounters all occurred near water, consistent with the general observation that this state-wide species prefers deciduous woodlands and is generally found near pools, ponds, or roadside ditches during the breeding season (Hulse et al. 2001). This species was not detected at the other three ACS sites, which also included areas with woods and suitable water for breeding. Yahner et al. (1999) found this species while testing survey methods at HOFU.

Northern Green Frog (*Rana clamitans melanota*)

This mid-sized frog was encountered seven times during the inventory, always during GHC surveys. It was primarily a resident of French Creek (71% of encounters) and was found once (14%) along a run (a tributary to the creek) and once (14%) in lowland forest near the confluence of French and Baptism Creeks. These observations are somewhat consistent with the known habitat requirements of this state-wide species. Northern green frogs are habitat generalists, using virtually any type of aquatic habitat, except for areas with very fast current (Hulse et al. 2001). It is not known why this species was not detected at the many other aquatic habitats surveyed at HOFU during the inventory. This species was also detected by Yahner et al. (1999).

Northern Spring Peeper (*Pseudacris crucifer crucifer*)

Peepers were detected six times, being heard once during GHC at ACS site 2 and heard five times during ACS at each of the five ACS sites. Habitat types were typically mixed (50% of encounters) or lowland forest (40%), with one encounter (10%) in an open wetland (flooded pasture). These encounters are consistent with the known ecology of this state-wide species, which typically spends the nonbreeding season in deciduous forests, swamps and adjacent marshy fields and meadows but moves more into nonwooded wet areas to reproduce (Hulse et al. 2001). Because it was found at all ACS calling sites, the peeper likely has a breeding population at HOFU. This species was also detected by Yahner et al. (1999).

Pickerel Frog (*Rana palustris*)

This frog was encountered 13 times in a range of habitat types. Primarily a resident of French Creek (46% of encounters) and various runs ((31%), it rarely occurred in terrestrial habitats, being found once in upland forest, once in an animal pen, and once in a corn field (8% each). This state-wide species is considered semi-aquatic, frequenting a wide variety of aquatic habitats during their spring breeding, but dispersing into more terrestrial habitats later in their activity season (Hulse et al. 2001). These terrestrial habitats tend to be mesic and include woods, open fields, and meadows. Thus, the spotty occurrence of this species in forest, an animal pen, and a corn field is consistent with nonbreeding habitat preferences. This species was detected primarily during GHC and only once heard during ACS (site 1). Yahner et al. (1999) found this species during their survey of HOFU.

Wood Frog (*Rana sylvatica*)

This mid-sized but secretive frog (Shaffer 1991) was somewhat of a habitat generalist. It was detected 13 times during the inventory, primarily in upland forest (38% of encounters) and along runs (23%), and less often in lowland forest (15%). Single encounters (8%) occurred in an open wetland (flooded pasture), a weedy field (power line right-of-way), and a corn field. All encounters were during GHC, with one exception. During an ACS, three individuals were found in a temporary pool in a pasture, which also contained eight egg masses. The pool dried completely a few days later and all eggs and tadpoles died. These observations on habitat use are consistent with the known ecology of this state-wide species, which prefers forested habitats during most of the year, but will use almost any nearby body of standing water to reproduce (Hulse et al. 2001). This species is an explosive breeder, meaning that most individuals in a given population come to the breeding pools nearly in synchrony and then disappear (Hulse et al. 2001). Thus, it can be easy to fail to detect this species unless the timing of the anura calling survey happens to coincide exactly with the short breeding event. Although the single breeding pool found in 2001 dried up, this species does not appear to be at risk. Encounters were

28

widespread at HOFU, and the range of body sizes (1.5-5.0 cm) suggests the population is doing well in terms of recruitment. Yahner et al. (1999) also reported this frog at HOFU.

Black Rat Snake (*Elaphe obsoleta obsoleta*)

This large snake was detected only once, during GHC, in upland forest near an ecotone. This species had been previously detected at HOFU (Yahner et al. 1999) and, based on its ecology and geographic distribution, was expected to be relatively common in the park. The range of this species includes the entire state, with reliable records from Chester and Berks Counties (Hulse et al. 2001). Where it does occur, it is typically relatively abundant (Palmer and Braswell 1995). Furthermore, the black rat snake is primarily an upland species preferring the ecotone between forest and field (Hulse et al. 2001). HOFU, with its mosaic of upland hardwood forest and various types of fields, should therefore provide ample suitable habitat. Nevertheless, despite many taxon-specific searches, this species appears to be relatively rare in the park.

Common Garter Snake (*Thamnophis sirtalis sirtalis*)

This common, mid-sized snake was the most frequently encountered snake in this inventory. The 20 sightings for this species occurred across a wide range of elevations, from the channel of French Creek to the slopes of Chestnut Hill. This snake also occupied the most habitat types of any species, giving it the highest HDI of any reptile or amphibian at HOFU. It was found primarily in upland forest (35%) and along French Creek (25%), and less often in lowland forest (15%) and along runs (10%). Single encounters (5% each) occurred at a large rocky slope, a weedy field (power line right-of-way), and the driveway to the Visitors' Center. These overall observations on habitat use are consistent with the literature on this species, as summarized by Hulse et al. (2001). They describe this state-wide species as the most common snake in the Northeast, with the largest range of habitats used by any snake.

Eastern Milk Snake (*Lampropeltis triangulum triangulum*)

This uncommon and secretive snake (Shaffer 1991) was encountered only once during this inventory, being found at the base of a wall on the west side of the Bethesda Church cemetery. This species is known to occur throughout the state, typically being found in open habitats, ecotones, around human structures, and in deciduous forest (Hulse et al. 2001). Thus, there appears to be abundant suitable habitat in the park. It is therefore possible that this species occurs at other locations in HOFU, where it may have been missed by the current inventory. This species was not detected by Yahner et al. (1999) and represents a new record for the park.

Northern Black Racer (*Coluber constrictor constrictor*)

This large snake represents a new record for the park. With 10 sightings, it was the second most abundant snake at HOFU, being found primarily in upland forest (40% of encounters) and pastures (30%). Two encounters (20%) occurred in a weedy field (power line right-of-way), and a single encounter (10%) occurred at a large rock pile. Encounter elevations ranged from the pasture above French Creek (approx. 140 m) to one of the highest points in the park on Chestnut Hill (approx. 274 m). These observations are consistent with known patterns of habitat use for this state-wide species, which prefers open woods, woods with rocky slopes, and open country, including meadows, old fields, utility rights-of-way, and farmland (Shaffer 1991; Hulse et al. 2001).

Northern Ringneck Snake (*Diadophis punctatus edwardsii*)

This small, secretive snake (Hulse et al. 2001) was encountered only five times, all in upland forest under cover (logs, rocks, and bark). This is similar to other studies, as summarized in Hulse et al. (2001), which describe the preferred habitats as being generally in or near to deciduous woods, including fields, rocky hillsides, and the shores of streams and rivers. Regardless of habitat type, the primary determinant of habitat quality for this state-wide species is the abundance of suitable cover objects, particularly rocks (Hulse et al. 2001). However, this species was always found at or above 160 m elevation and, thus, appears not to prefer the lower regions in the park. This species was found by Yahner et al. (1999) and likely occurs throughout the park in upland areas with an abundance of loose surface rock.

Northern Water Snake (*Nerodia sipedon sipedon*)

This aquatic snake was encountered eight times, primarily along French Creek (50% of encounters) and runs (25%), with single encounters (12% each) in upland forest near a spring and in an open wetland (flooded pasture) where an individual was found during an ACS. These sightings are consistent with the known habitat preferences of this species in Pennsylvania, where this state-wide species inhabits most aquatic and semi-aquatic habitats (Hulse et al. 2001). The northern water snake was the third most frequently encountered snake of this inventory, consistent with the assertion by Hulse et al. (2001) that this is one of the most common snakes in the Northeast. This reptile was also detected by Yahner et al. (1999), and the range of body sizes (21.5-45.0 cm SVL) found during the current inventory suggests a breeding population is supported at HOFU.

Common Musk Turtle (*Sternotherus odoratus*)

This small, inconspicuous, aquatic turtle (Shaffer 1991) represents a new record for HOFU. The park is just inside the geographic range for this species, which extends to the northern boundary of Berks County (Hulse et al. 2001). There exist reliable recent records for this species very close to HOFU from Chester and Berks Counties (Hulse et al. 2001). This turtle was detected five times, with four encounters in French Creek (80% of encounters) and one individual (20%) found in the outflow from the water wheel at the base of the Cast House. The water wheel receives water from Hopewell Lake via the west head race; this water then flows a short distance into French Creek after exiting the Cast House. French Creek has some sections that appear to provide ideal habitat for this turtle, which is known to be fond of slower waters with soft mud bottoms (Behler and King 1996). This little reptile might also occur at HOFU in several of the runs and flooded areas in lowland forest, which also have muddy bottoms.

Common Snapping Turtle (*Chelydra serpentina serpentina*)

The largest of the native turtles of the Commonwealth (Hulse et al. 2001), this reptile was found only once during the inventory. The single encounter was of a very young turtle with a carapace length of only 3.2 cm. Hatchlings in Pennsylvania range from 2.2-3.1 cm and emerge from the egg from August-October (Hulse et al. 2001). Thus, this May encounter was most likely a hatchling from the previous year. The common snapping turtle is a carnivore, found throughout the Commonwealth, and is a habitat generalist that can be found in almost every freshwater habitat (Hulse et al. 2001). However, the failure to detect any large juveniles or adults at HOFU suggests that this species might be reproducing outside the park, most likely in Hopewell Lake, which releases water into French Creek. Yahner et al. (1999) also found the common snapping turtle in the park.

Eastern Box Turtle (*Terrapene carolina carolina*)

This terrestrial turtle was encountered 10 times at HOFU, making it the most abundant of the five turtle species detected by this inventory. Box turtles were widely distributed throughout the park and were found primarily in upland forest (60% of encounters) and hay fields within 15 m of upland forest (30%). A single encounter occurred in wet lowland forest (10%). These observations are consistent with other reports from Pennsylvania, where this species is found throughout most of the lower two-thirds of the state (Hulse et al. 2001). Eastern box turtles are the only terrestrial turtles in the Northeast, most frequently found in deciduous forest and ecotones between forest and fields. During dry spells, however, they may move into more mesic habitats, including marshy areas (Hulse et al. 2001). This intelligent turtle (Tyning 1990) was also detected by Yahner et al. (1999).

Red-eared Slider (*Trachemys scripta elegans*)

This exotic turtle was detected twice during this inventory and represents a new park record. Both encounters likely involved the same individual, which was first caught in the sheep pen and then later seen nearby in French Creek. The slider is not native to Pennsylvania and is not mentioned as being an established resident in the state by McCoy (1982), Shaffer (1991), or Hulse et al. (2001). However, reports from West Virginia (Green and Pauley 1987) and the Delmarva Peninsula (White and White 2002), which also support introduced populations, indicate this turtle has a preference for quiet water with a mud bottom and abundant vegetation. French Creek offers such habitat in several places, and so might the nearby Hopewell Lake, which is just a few meters outside the park boundaries. The original source of colonists is most likely pets that escaped or were released into the wild (Conant and Collins 1998), and nearby Valley Forge National Historical Park (about 35 km away) appears to support a large, successfully reproducing population (Tiebout 2003).

Wood Turtle (*Clemmys insculpta*)

This mid-sized semiaquatic turtle (White and White 2002) represents a new record for HOFU. This reptile was encountered four times, twice along French Creek and twice in an open wetland immediately adjacent to the creek. The latter two encounters were of two adults copulating, and twice during the inventory adult females were observed laying eggs in the charcoal pits adjacent to the Charcoal Hearth, though one nest was apparently preyed upon by raccoons (*Procyon lotor*, Jeffrey Collins, pers. comm.). It is not surprising to find a reproductive population of wood turtles at HOFU. The park lies well within the range of this species, and there are reliable recent records from both Berks and Chester Counties (Hulse et al. 2001). In addition, HOFU contains ample suitable habitat, which Hulse et al. (2001) characterized as open meadows, bogs, forest, old fields, and small creeks and streams. Kaufmann (1992) found that wood turtles in central Pennsylvania prefer alder thickets, open meadows, and corn fields.

Habitat Use by Species

The two species that appeared to be habitat generalists, common garter snake and wood frog, were not particularly abundant animals (3.6 and 2.3% of total encounters, respectively). This is in contrast to findings at VAFO, where herpetofauna that were habitat generalists also tended to be among the most abundant species in the park (Tiebout 2003). Similar to the results of the VAFO inventory, the six HOFU species that were found in just a single habitat type also tended to be among the least abundant species (Tiebout 2003). This restriction of some species to a single habitat type indicates that even habitat types with low species richness can be critical to supporting the full range of herpetofauna species in the park. For example, buildings and associated grounds yielded only five species, but two of these (longtail salamander, eastern milk snake) were not found in any other habitat types. In particular, both of these species were found in or around historical structures, suggesting that these park resources could play a role as key herpetofauna habitat.

Species Richness by Habitat Type

It was determined that four of the 14 habitat types were the most species-rich and collectively contained representatives of all but two of the 25 species found in the inventory. These four species-rich habitat types should be considered the most important in supporting a rich herpetofauna assemblage in the park: upland forest, runs, lowland forest, and French Creek. In addition, the edges of various types of fields (defined as within 15 m of a forest or French Creek), although not recorded as a discrete habitat type, also contained a diverse array of reptiles and amphibians. Edges of pastures, hay fields, corn fields, and weedy fields yielded seven species (eastern American toad, common garter snake, eastern box turtle, northern black racer, pickerel frog, red-backed salamander, and wood frog). Two of these habitat types are mowed or harvested annually (hay and corn fields), one is cut less often (weedy field under the power line right-of-way), and one is subject to the minor disturbance of grazing (pasture). The only known animal mortality assumed to be associated with these human-related activities was a single eastern box turtle apparently killed by a hay cutter in field 10.

Species on the Predicted List Not Detected

Eastern Hellbender (*Cryptobranchus a. alleganiensis*) - Probable Nonresident

This large salamander has not been reported at HOFU. It was originally put on the predicted list because, according to Yahner et al. (1999), the park fell within its geographic range. However, a more recent range map indicates that this species has not been historically found in Chester, Montgomery, or Berks Counties, and HOFU appears to be completely outside its current geographic distribution (Hulse et al. 2001). Accordingly, the eastern hellbender is almost certainly not a resident of the park.

Eastern Newt (also known as Red-spotted Newt, *Notophthalmus viridescens viridescens*) - Probable Current Resident

This salamander was recently detected at HOFU by Yahner et al. (1999), the park is well within the geographic range of this species, and the park contains ample suitable habitat. Eastern newts are common throughout the Commonwealth, with reliable recent records near the park in Chester and Berks Counties (Hulse et al. 2001). This amphibian can be found in a number of aquatic habitats, including temporary and permanent ponds, lakes, and slowly moving streams and creeks (Hulse et al. 2001). In addition, these newts appear to prefer areas in or near to woods (Hulse et al. 2001). Thus, with its mix of forest habitat types and abundance of creeks, runs, and vernal pools, HOFU appears to contain more than enough ideal habitat to support this species.

Jefferson Salamander (*Ambystoma jeffersonianum*) - Indeterminate

This secretive species (Hulse et al. 2001) was not found by other investigators, not reported on HOFU WOCs, and has no recent reliable records from Chester or Berks Counties (Hulse et al. 2001). Nevertheless, the park does fall within the general geographic range for this species (Shaffer 1991; Hulse et al. 2001) and does contain suitable upland forest habitat with some nearby wet areas for reproduction (Hulse et al. 2001). Acid precipitation may play a role in limiting the distribution of this and other species of *Ambystoma* (Hulse et al. 2001), although the congeneric spotted salamander appears to be doing well in the park. Accordingly, the status of this salamander remains indeterminate.

Marbled Salamander (*Ambystoma opacum*) - Indeterminate

Although this salamander was not found by other investigators and not reported on HOFU WOCs, there are recent reliable records from both Berks County and nearby Montgomery County (Hulse et al. 2001). HOFU is thus well within the species current geographic range, and the park contains ample suitable upland forest habitat. However, this species may face the same limitations described above for the Jefferson salamander and its status in the park remains indeterminate.

Mountain Dusky Salamander (*Desmognathus f. fuscus*) - Probable Nonresident

This salamander has not been reported at HOFU. Originally put on the predicted list based on range maps (Yahner et al. 1999), new data now indicate that this species has not been documented in Chester or Berks Counties, nor in any of the adjacent counties (Hulse et al. 2001), and HOFU is well outside the range of this amphibian. Accordingly, the this species is almost certainly not a resident of the park.

Northern Spring Salamander (*Gyrinophilus porphyriticus porphyriticus*) - Indeterminate

This species was not found by other investigators and not reported on HOFU WOCs, and it is not clear if the park falls within the geographic range for this species. According to Hulse et al. (2001), there are recent records from Chester County and nearby Lancaster County; thus HOFU falls within the current range. According to somewhat older sources (Shaffer 1991; Petranka 1998), the park is just outside the geographic range. The park does contain some suitably cool, clean springs that could support this species (Shaffer 1991), but exhaustive searches of these habitats failed to detect any individuals. Accordingly, this habitat-specialist (Hulse et al. 2001) remains indeterminate in status.

Valley and Ridge Salamander (*Plethodon hoffmani*) - Probable Nonresident

This salamander has not been reported at HOFU. It was originally put on the predicted list because the park appeared to fall within its geographic range (Yahner et al. 1999). However, the most current range map (Hulse et al. 2001) indicates that this species has not historically been found in Chester or Berks Counties, or in any of the adjacent counties. Because HOFU is now considered well outside the range for this species, the valley and ridge salamander should be considered a nonresident of the park.

Bullfrog (*Rana catesbeiana*) - Indeterminate

This large frog of state-wide distribution (Hulse et al. 2001) has never been documented at HOFU. This species begins to call in late April and may continue calling until the middle or end of June (Hulse et al. 2001). If present in HOFU, it could have been heard during ACS number 3 (23 May 2001) or 4 (22 June 2001). Hulse et al. (2001) describe its required habitat in Pennsylvania as being permanent bodies of water, including ponds, lakes, streams, and rivers. In streams and rivers it appears to prefer slow-moving sections. HOFU has very few such habitats, with the exception of two slow sections of French Creek where the channel widens. One section is near the animal pens and is quite shallow, the other is nearer to Hopewell Lake in the vicinity of the vernal pools at ACS site 1 and is larger and deeper. A large frog (ca. 17-18 cm body length) with a very thick body was observed by HOFU Chief Ranger Jeffrey Collins near these vernal pools (J. Collins, pers. comm. 27 April 2001). The average body length for Pennsylvania bullfrogs is 11.9 cm (Hulse et al. 2001), making them the largest frog in the Commonwealth. The next largest frog in Pennsylvania is the northern green frog, which has a maximum body length of 10.8 cm (Conant and Collins 1991). Thus, the large frog seen by Collins was very possibly a bullfrog, perhaps having come from Hopewell Lake, which is approximately 150 m from ACS site 1. Accordingly, this species is considered indeterminate. Individuals may occasionally enter HOFU from nearby Hopewell Lake, but there is no evidence of reproduction occurring in the park.

Eastern Spadefoot Toad (*Scaphiopus holbrooki holbrooki*) - Probable Nonresident

Although this species appeared on the predicted species list of Yahner et al. (1999), it has never been documented in the park. More recent, detailed information on its distribution within Pennsylvania (Hulse et al. 2001) indicates that HOFU is completely outside its range. Furthermore, the spadefoot prefers habitats with sandy soils that are located along floodplains and in agricultural fields ((Hulse et al. 2001). These types of habitats are virtually absent from HOFU, with the exception of one small sandy area of 1-2 ha along the drainage of Baptism Creek, approximately 100 m north of Hopewell Road. Accordingly, it is unlikely that this species has ever inhabited the park, and it is considered a probable nonresident.

Fowler's Toad (*Bufo fowleri*) - Probable Nonresident

This species has never been documented at HOFU. These toads typically begin calling in mid-May and continue through late June (Hulse et al. 2001). Accordingly, if this species were present in HOFU, it could have been heard during ACS 3 (23 May 2001) or 4 (22 June 2001). Although the park does fall well within its geographic range, and there are reliable records very close to the park from northern Chester County and southern Berks County (Hulse et al. 2001), HOFU does not appear to contain any suitable habitat. Fowler's toad is a habitat specialist, preferring open habitats with well-drained sandy or gravelly soils (Hulse et al. 2001). Thus, these toads tend to be found near streams and rivers and away from upland or wooded habitats. As noted above (see "Eastern Spadefoot"), the only sandy or gravelly area in the park is along Baptism Creek, and this area is a heavily forested upland habitat. Therefore, this species likely does not occur in HOFU and is considered a probable nonresident.

Northern Cricket Frog - Indeterminate

This diminutive species has never been documented at HOFU. This species is known to chorus in Pennsylvania from May through late July (Hulse et al. 2001), so it could have been detected during ACS 3 (23 May 2001) or 4 (22 June 2001), if it occurs in the park. Although HOFU is well within the range of this species, and there are reliable records from eastern Montgomery County (Hulse et al. 2001), HOFU may be lacking in suitable habitat. Unlike many other small frogs in the region, northern cricket frogs remain near water throughout the year, preferring still or slow-moving permanent water in open habitats and avoiding heavily wooded areas (Shaffer 1991; Hulse et al. 2001). The only such habitat in HOFU occurs along French Creek in the vicinity of the sheep pen, an area surveyed from ACS site 2 and visited frequently during GHC. According to Shaffer (1991), these frogs make use of emergent vegetation, but this section of French Creek has relatively sparse vegetation. Thus, HOFU might provide only suboptimal habitat. This small anuran is therefore considered indeterminate in status.

Northern Leopard Frog (*Rana pipiens*) - Probable Current Resident

Previously documented at HOFU (Yahner et al. 1999), this species was not detected during the current inventory. This species is known to call in Pennsylvania from March until May or June, so it could have been heard during any of the four ACS visits. HOFU appears to contain some suitable habitat, both for breeding and nonbreeding seasons. Reproduction typically occurs in temporary pools formed in meadows and fields, with a preference for warm, shallow water in open areas with emergent vegetation (Hulse et al. 2001). Such habitat occurs in three general areas of the park, including the extreme western end of field 6b (covered by ACS site 2), the open marshy area between Harrison Lloyd Road and Bethesda Road (not covered by any ACS site), and a similar area between field 12 and Baptism Creek (covered by ACS site 4). During the nonbreeding season, leopard frogs are known to occur in a variety of habitats, e.g., vegetated borders of still or slow-moving waters, but they can also move into surrounding fields, meadows and woodlands if it is not too dry (Hulse et al. 2001). Such habitats at HOFU include the breeding areas described above, plus much of the lowland forest (especially when wet), as well as the margins of fields nearest wet areas (especially fields 6a, 6b, 7, 10, and 12). HOFU appears to be near the southeastern limit of the range of this species in Pennsylvania, with one reliable record from southern Berks County (Hulse et al. 2001). Thus, it is possible the park contains a marginal population that is abundant some years but sparse in other years.

Upland Chorus Frog (*Pseudacris triseriata feriarum*) - Indeterminate

This species has never been documented at HOFU. In Pennsylvania, it is known to call from early March to mid-May (Hulse et al. 2001) and, thus, could potentially have been detected by ACS numbers 1 and 2. According to Shaffer (1991), HOFU lies outside the geographic range of this species. However, according to Hulse et al. (2001), the park is inside the range, although the nearest reliable record is from extreme northern Montgomery County, approximately 30 km from HOFU. It appears HOFU offers abundant habitat for both reproductive and nonreproductive activity. For reproduction, upland chorus frogs favor temporary pools in almost any type of habitat, as well as roadside ditches (Hulse et al. 2001). HOFU contains a variety of temporary wetlands and has a large roadside ditch along the east side of PA Route 345. During the nonbreeding season, this small anuran favors densely vegetated habitats, including wooded areas, marshes, and meadows, and any of these can be either in wet or dry areas (Hulse et al. 2001). Again, HOFU appears to provide many such areas with dense vegetation, particularly the marshy area between fields 6a and 6b, the lowland forest east of fields 6b and 7, the open marshy area between Harrison Lloyd Road and Bethesda Road, and a similar area between field 12 and Baptism Creek. Although this species has not been found at HOFU, the park contains suitable habitat and may or may not be within the geographic range for this anuran. Thus, the status of the upland chorus frog remains inconclusive and must be considered indeterminate.

Five-lined Skink (*Eumeces fasciatus*) - Possible Extirpated Resident

This lizard has never been recorded at HOFU, yet the species is widely distributed throughout the lower two-thirds of the state and has a reliable record from northern Berks County (Shaffer 1991; Hulse et al. 2001). Because HOFU contains an abundance of suitable open habitat with fallen logs, rocks, and debris from abandoned human habitations (Hulse et al. 2001), it is likely this species once occurred in the park. The most likely areas where this lizard could have been found include the stone fence rows along the margins of fields, the power line right-of-way along the northeastern boundary, rocky areas along the eastern side of Mount Pleasure, open rocky areas at the extreme southern boundary, and the hillside containing the Anthracite Furnace. Because there have been no reports of any lizards at HOFU, and because lizards can be relatively easy to detect during visual surveys (H. Tiebout, pers. obs.), it is unlikely that this species currently inhabits the park.

Northern Fence Lizard (*Sceloporus undulatus hyacinthinus*) - Possible Extirpated Resident

This small reptile has never been reported at HOFU. However, the park lies well inside the current geographic range of this species, and there is a reliable record from extreme southern Berks County near the park (Hulse et al. 2001). HOFU appears to provide ample habitat consisting of open woodland, rocky outcrops, and fallen snags (Shaffer 1991; Hulse et al. 2001). Areas that may have supported this species in the past are those described above (see "Five-lined Skink"). Because there have been no reports of any lizards at HOFU, it is likely that this species no longer inhabits the park. However, it possibly may have been a resident historically.

Eastern Hognose Snake (*Heterodon platirhinos*) - Probable Nonresident

This elusive, fossorial species (Hulse et al. 2001) has not been reported at HOFU. Although the park does lie well within this species geographic distribution, which includes reliable records from northern Berks County and extreme northern Chester County (Hulse et al. 2001), HOFU probably contains very little suitable habitat. This snake is known to prefer grasslands and open woodland, particularly those with dry sandy soil (Shaffer 1991; Hulse et al. 2001). As discussed above (see "Fowler's Toad"), sandy soils are uncommon at HOFU. The one such area located during this inventory is in closed-canopy forest and, being in the floodplain of Baptism Creek, has relatively damp soil. Accordingly, it is unlikely that this species has ever been present at HOFU.

Eastern Ribbon Snake (*Thamnophis sauritus sauritus*) - Indeterminate

This snake has never been reported at HOFU. However, the park is well within the range of this semi-aquatic, semi-arboreal reptile, and there are recent, reliable records from Chester County and from northern Montgomery County near HOFU (Hulse et al. 2001). In addition, the park contains a small amount of suitable habitat of the types described by Hulse et al. (2001): rocky hillsides, grassy fields, and forests, each of which should be near standing or flowing permanent water. Regions in the park that could potentially support this species include the areas immediately adjacent to French Creek and Baptism Creek. Thus, the likelihood of this species being a current or historical resident is small, and its status remains indeterminate.

Eastern Earth Snake (*Virginia valeriae valeriae*) - Possible Extirpated Resident

This snake, which is seldom encountered except after heavy rains (Hulse et al. 2001), has never been reported at HOFU. The park is situated within or near to the former geographic range of this species (Shaffer 1991; Hulse et al. 2001). In addition, the park appears to have suitable habitat for this occupant of deciduous forest, which can be found under logs, rocks, and other surface debris (Hulse et al. 2001). However, although there are historical records from western Montgomery County and southern Berks County near the park, the populations in southeastern Pennsylvania are now believed to have been extirpated due to development (Hulse et al. 2001). Consequently, based on geography, availability of habitat, and the fate of other populations in southeastern Pennsylvania, this species should be considered a possible extirpated resident.

Eastern Worm Snake (*Carphophis amoenus amoenus*) - Indeterminate

This secretive, fossorial snake (Hulse et al. 2001) has not been reported at HOFU. The park is well within the current geographic range of this species (Shaffer 1991; Hulse et al. 2001), although the nearest reliable record is from extreme southern Chester County, approximately 56 km from the park. HOFU contains some of its preferred habitat, which is known to include damp hilly woodlands and grasslands (Shaffer 1991). However, ideal habitat for this burrowing reptile may require the presence of moderately sandy soil (Hulse et al. 2001), which is not common at HOFU (see "Eastern Spadefoot Toad" above). In addition, because this animal spends so much of its life underground and is seldom found in the open, detection of this reptile can be very difficult (Hulse et al. 2001). Accordingly, this reptile remains indeterminate in status.

Northern Brown Snake (*Storeria dekayi dekayi*) - Probable Current Resident

This small, inconspicuous snake, which can be very abundant locally (Ernst and Barbour 1989), has not been reported from the park. However, HOFU is well within the geographic range for this species (Shaffer 1991; Hulse et al. 2001), with reliable records from southern Berks County and western Montgomery County. In addition, it is known to occur in a wide variety of habitats, from dry hillsides to wet areas around ponds and lakes, provided there is an abundance of cover objects (Shaffer 1991; Hulse et al. 2001). Thus, HOFU appears to offer ample suitable habitat for this species. Consequently, it seems likely that this species resides in HOFU but was not detected by the current inventory.

Northern Copperhead (*Agkistrodon contortrix mokasen*) - Probable Current Resident

This mid-sized snake, which is the only venomous reptile predicted to occur at HOFU, has never been documented at the park. This is surprising, because HOFU is well within the geographic range for this species, which includes the entire southern two-thirds of the Commonwealth (Shaffer 1991; Hulse et al. 2001), and reliable records are known from Chester, Montgomery, Berks, and Lancaster Counties. Furthermore, the park contains ample suitable habitat, described as hillsides with deciduous forest and rocky outcrops, associated fields and clearings, stone walls, piles of rock, and farms (Shaffer 1991; Hulse et al. 2001). In a special effort to detect this snake, an expert on northern copperheads, Mark J. Johnson from Villanova University, was contracted to search for this species. On 13 September 2001, he and two assistants spent a full day in the park searching the most likely basking habitats, which often serve as congregation sites for this species at this time of year (Tiebout 2003, H. Tiebout, pers. obs.). The areas searched included the rock hilltop at the extreme southern boundary of the park (and an adjacent rocky slope in State Game Land No. 43), the eastern slope of Mount Pleasant, a rocky slope south of the intersection of PA Route 345 and Park Road, and rocky areas between Lenape Trail and the power line right-of-way. Although four snakes were detected (three northern black racers, one common garter snake), no northern copperheads were found. As a point of reference, this species was detected at nearby VAFO in September in similar habitats during similar weather in 1999, 2000, and 2001 (Tiebout 2003; M. Myers pers. comm.). M. Johnson concluded that the habitats surveyed were very suitable for northern copperheads and suggested that this species likely occurred in the park despite not being found during the current inventory.

Northern Redbelly Snake (*Storeria occipitomaculata occipitomaculata*) - Probable Nonresident

This small snake has not been reported at HOFU. It was originally put on the predicted list, because the park appeared to fall within its geographic range (Shaffer 1991). However, a more recent range map indicates that this species has not historically been found in Chester, Montgomery, or southern Berks Counties (Hulse et al. 2001), and HOFU is not included in the range of this snake. Accordingly, the northern redbelly snake is almost certainly not a resident of the park.

Rough Green Snake (*Opheodrys aestivus*) - Probable Nonresident

HOFU has no record of this rare species, which is listed as threatened by the Commonwealth (Wild Resource Conservation Fund 1995). It was put on the predicted list based on the range map in Shaffer (1991). However, a more recent range map (Hulse et al. 2001) presents only a single reliable record from southeastern Pennsylvania (extreme southwestern tip of Chester County), suggesting that HOFU may actually be outside the current range for this snake. It should therefore be considered a nonresident of the park.

Queen Snake (*Regina septemvittata*) - Indeterminate

Taxon-specific searches (see "Sampling Design" above) for this species focused on areas of the park that appeared to be the best habitat for this mid-sized, highly aquatic snake (Shaffer 1991; Hulse et al. 2001). These target areas included sections of French Creek and its immediate tributaries where there was abundant loose rock along the banks and/or low vegetation overhanging the water. Queen snakes were not detected at HOFU, despite ample available habitat and the fact that the park is well within the geographic range for this species, with a reliable record from northern Chester County near the park (Shaffer 1991; Hulse et al. 2001). This species was detected numerous times in similar habitats along Valley Creek at VAFO using the same searching techniques. However, it has never been documented at HOFU, suggesting it might be absent or present only in very low density at the park.

Bog Turtle (*Clemmys muhlenbergii*) - Indeterminate

This federally threatened and Pennsylvania endangered species (Wild Resource Conservation Fund 1995; White and White 2002) has not been documented at HOFU. It was put on the predicted list because the park falls within the geographic distribution of this species, and there are numerous recent and historical records from Chester, Montgomery, and Berks Counties (Wild Resource Conservation Fund 1995; Hulse et al. 2001). In addition, a population is currently being monitored in Warwick County Park (R. Zappalorti, pers. comm.), about 6 km south of HOFU. In the course of the inventory, several areas within HOFU were identified that could potentially support bog turtles (Figure 3), based on the presence of suitable hydric conditions (open-canopy wetlands, clear water flowing over soft mud bottom, wet pastures) and associated plant species (tussock sedge [*Carex stricta*], spotted jewelweed [*Impatiens capensis*], red maple [*Acer rubrum*], These areas were subjected to several taxon-specific searches during spring 2000. No bog turtles were detected, but because this species can be very difficult to detect (U. S. Fish and Wildlife Service 2001, see discussion under "Habitats of Special Concern" below), it may be present in the park.

Eastern Painted Turtle (*Chrysemys picta picta*) - Probable Current Resident

This mid-sized aquatic turtle (Shaffer 1991) has previously been documented at HOFU (Yahner et al. 1999) but was not detected during the current inventory. This common turtle with a state-wide distribution has reliable records from Chester, Montgomery, Berks, and Lancaster Counties (Hulse et al. 2001). It is considered a habitat generalist, being found in almost any aquatic habitat except bogs, swift-flowing streams that lack quiet pools, and standing water that lacks aquatic vegetation ((Behler and King 1996; Hulse et al. 2001). There are two sections of French Creek that appear suitable for this species (see description in "Bullfrog" above). In addition, eastern painted turtles also likely inhabit nearby Hopewell Lake and may occasionally enter HOFU via French Creek, which exits the lake and enters the park.

Red-bellied Turtle (*Pseudemys rubriventris*) - Probable Nonresident

This Pennsylvania threatened species (Wild Resource Conservation Fund 1995) has not been documented at HOFU. It does occur nearby in Phoenixville, only 20 km southeast of HOFU, where it is abundant and apparently reproducing in the canals that parallel the Schuylkill River (Tiebout 2003). Despite their close proximity to the park, red-bellied turtles likely do not inhabit HOFU because of lack of suitable habitat. This species is known to prefer large, deep bodies of water with dense aquatic vegetation. Such habitats are absent from HOFU, so this species should be considered a probable nonresident.

Spotted Turtle (*Clemmys gutatta*) - Probable Current Resident

This aquatic reptile has previously been reported at HOFU but was not detected in the current inventory. The park is well within the current range for this species, which includes reliable records from Berks County and northern Chester County near the park (Hulse et al. 2001). HOFU contains suitable habitat in the form of wet meadows, swamps, and shallow mud-bottomed streams (Shaffer 1991; Hulse et al. 2001). Failure to find this species during this inventory may suggest that it occurs at relatively low density within the park.

Figure 3. Map of potential bog turtle habitat at Hopewell Furnace National Historic Site. These areas were determined to be appropriate habitat based on Shaffer (1991) and Hulse et al. (2001).

N

| HOFU Boundary |
| Potential Bog Turtle Habitat |

0   500   1000   1500   2000 Meters

Revised Predicted Species List and Future Inventory Needs

The 25 species detected plus the six species determined to be probable current residents yields a revised predicted species list of 35 species (Table 9). Thus, the inventory detected approximately 81% of the likely resident species at HOFU. Additional taxon-specific surveys should be conducted in the habitats previously identified for each species (see "Species on the Predicted List Not Detected" above) in an attempt to confirm the presence of these six probable current residents.

Future Indicator Species for Major Habitat Types

Four habitat types were found to be the most species-rich (upland forest, lowland forest, runs, French Creek), supporting 92% of the species detected in this inventory. The following species are likely candidates to serve as indicator species of the ecological health of these four habitat types. For the purposes of this report, the term ecological health is considered synonymous with biological integrity, as defined by Karr (1997):

> Biological integrity is the ability to support and maintain a balanced, integrated, adaptive biological system having the full range of elements and processes expected in the natural habitat of a region.

These species were selected based on criteria suggested by Seigel and Simons (1995) and Noss (1997): their relative abundance (and hence ecological importance), dependence upon the given habitat type, ease of monitoring, and potential sensitivity to environmental change.

Upland Forest

Red-backed salamander. -- This is one of the most abundant and ecologically important vertebrates in northeastern deciduous forest (Burton and Likens 1975). Because it is easy to monitor and likely sensitive to environmental change, it is one of the designated indicator species for monitoring under the new federal Terrestrial Salamander Monitoring Program of the U. S. Geological Survey (USGS; Droege et al. 1997).

Lowland Forest

Red-backed salamander. -- See justification in "Upland Forest" above.

Four-toed salamander. -- This species was encountered only in lowland forest or along runs in lowland forest. A habitat-specialist, this amphibian is at risk from development and known to be vulnerable to local extirpation from human activities (Shaffer 1991; Hulse et al. 2001).

Runs

Northern dusky salamander and northern two-lined salamander. -- Both of these species are stream salamanders, meaning they are dependent upon small streams for reproduction and for

Table 9. Predicted list of amphibians and reptiles at Hopewell Furnace National Historic Site, including all species detected by the current inventory, plus six species not detected during the current inventory but considered probable current residents.

Group	Common Name	Scientific Name	ITIS TSN[1]	Found in Current Inventory[2]	Probable Current Resident[3]
Salamanders					
	Eastern (Red-spotted) Newt	*Notophthalmus v. viridescens*	173616		X
	Four-toed Salamander	*Hemidactylium scutatum*	173678	X	
	Longtail Salamander	*Eurycea l. longicauda*	208310	X	
	Northern Dusky Salamander	*Desmognathus f. fuscus*	173634	X	
	Northern Red Salamander	*Pseudotriton r. ruber*	173681	X	
	Northern Two-lined Salamander	*Eurycea bislineata*	173685	X	
	Red-backed Salamander	*Plethodon cinereus*	173649	X	
	Slimy Salamander	*Plethodon glutinosus*	173650	X	
	Spotted Salamander	*Ambystoma maculatum*	173590	X	
Toads & Frogs					
	Eastern American Toad	*Bufo a. americanus*	173474	X	
	Eastern Gray Treefrog	*Hyla versicolor*	173503	X	
	Northern Green Frog	*Rana clamitans melanota*	173439	X	
	Northern Leopard Frog	*Rana pipiens*	173443		X
	Northern Spring Peeper	*Pseudacris c. crucifer*	207304	X	
	Pickerel Frog	*Rana palustris*	173435	X	
	Wood Frog	*Rana sylvatica*	173440	X	
Snakes					
	Black Rat Snake	*Elaphe o. obsoleta*	174178	X	
	Common Garter Snake	*Thamnophis s. sirtalis*	174137	X	
	Eastern Milk Snake	*Lampropeltis t. triangulum*	209242	X	
	Northern Black Racer	*Coluber c. constrictor*	174170	X	
	Northern Brown Snake	*Storeria d. dekayi*	174130		X
	Northern Copperhead	*Agkistrodon contortrix mokasen*	174297		X
	Northern Ringneck Snake	*Diadophis punctatus edwardsii*	209171	X	
	Northern Water Snake	*Nerodia s. sipedon*	174253	X	
Turtles					
	Common Musk Turtle	*Sternotherus odoratus*	173758	X	
	Common Snapping Turtle	*Chelydra s. serpentina*	173753	X	
	Eastern Box Turtle	*Terrapene c. carolina*	173777	X	
	Eastern Painted Turtle	*Chrysemys p. picta*	173784		X
	Red-eared Slider	*Trachemys scripta elegans*	173823	X	
	Spotted Turtle	*Clemmys guttata*	173771		X
	Wood Turtle	*Clemmys insculpta*	173772	X	

(1)   Integrated Taxonomic Information System - Taxonomic Serial Number (from http://www.itis.usda.gov/)

(2)   See section in text entitled "Species Detected" for complete description.

(3)   See section in text entitled "Species on the Predicted List Not Detected" for complete description.

long-term population survival. These species are considered to be excellent ecological indicators of small stream ecological health and are the focus of a new monitoring program under the Amphibian Research and Monitoring Initiative (ARMI) program of the USGS (Jung 2002a).

French Creek

Northern green frog and pickerel frog. -- These were two of the most commonly encountered species found in and immediately adjacent to French Creek, an Exceptional Value Pennsylvania Scenic River that was placed on the Conservation River Registry in 1998 (Heister and Geer 2001). Both species were more common along French Creek than in any other habitat types. Because of their ease of monitoring and sensitivity to environmental change, these species (and other anurans) have been identified as key indicator species by the USGS NAAMP (Weir 2001).

Species of Special Concern

Four-toed Salamander

See justification as an indicator species for lowland forest above.

Spotted Salamander

This species is dependent upon vernal pools and other ephemeral water sources for reproduction and has been designated an indicator species of the ecological health of vernal pools by the USGS under the new ARMI program (Jung 2002b).

Red-eared Slider

The red-eared slider is an exotic, invasive species in Pennsylvania (Somma et al. 2002) and is considered by the World Conservation Union to be one of the 100 worst invasive alien species in the world (Lowe et al. [no date]). With an omnivorous diet and ability to wander far from water and quickly colonize newly available habitats, this species already poses the threat of out-competing some native North American turtle species for food resources (Somma et al. 2002). Red-eared sliders were the most frequently encountered turtle species at VAFO, which supports a large breeding population in Valley Creek and the Schuylkill River (Tiebout 2003). This VAFO population is only about 24 km from HOFU; the Schuylkill River flows within about 4 km of HOFU. Accordingly, this species should be eliminated from HOFU before a breeding population becomes established, and the park should be carefully monitored to prevent recolonization by new individuals.

Wood Turtle

This semi-aquatic turtle appears to be maintaining a small, reproducing population at HOFU. However, this attractive reptile is especially prone to over-collecting for personal ownership and for the commercial pet trade, as well as to mortality on roadways, both of which put this turtle at risk of extirpation in the Commonwealth (Hulse et al. 2001). Several states have already listed this species as endangered or threatened, and populations in Pennsylvania should be closely monitored (Hulse et al. 2001).

Habitats of Special Concern

Potential Bog Turtle Habitat

Four general areas were identified as potential habitat for this federally and state listed turtle (Figure 3). Although these areas were surveyed for this rare reptile, none was found. However, because these animals can be so difficult to detect, failure to find them does not verify that they are absent from a site (U. S. Fish and Wildlife Service 2001). Accordingly, a State or federal certified bog turtle surveyor should be brought in to reevaluate the suitability of these areas and, if appropriate, search for this species.

Vernal Pools

These temporary wetlands are important breeding areas for wood frogs, spotted salamanders (see justification in "Species of Special Concern" above) and other amphibians, as well as several important invertebrates. It is recommended that vernal pool monitoring should be conducted following the ARMI protocols (Jung 2002b).

Literature Cited

Behler, J. L., and F. W. King. 1996. The Audubon Society field guide to North American reptiles and amphibians. Alfred A. Knopf, Inc., New York, NY. 743 pp.

Bowersox, T. W., and D. S. Larrick. 1999. Long-term vegetation monitoring of forested ecosystems at Hopewell National Historic Site and Valley Forge National Historical Park. Technical Report NPS/PHSO/NRTR-99/077. 75 pp.

Burton, T. M. and G. E. Likens. 1975. Salamander populations and biomass in the Hubbard Brook Experimental Forest, New Hampshire. Copeia 1975:541-546.

Campbell, H. W., and Christman, S. P. 1982. Field techniques for herpetofaunal community analysis. Pp. 193-200 *In* N. J. Scott (Ed.) Herpetological communities. USDI Fish and Wildlife Service, Research Report 13.

Conant, R. and J. T. Collins. 1998. A field guide to the reptiles and amphibians: eastern and central north America. Third edition. Houghton Mifflin Company, Boston, Massachusetts. 616 pp.

Delaware Valley Orienteering Association. 1992. French Creek East Orienteering Map, including portions of French Creek State Park and Hopewell Village Historic Site, DVOA, 14 Lake Drive, Spring City, PA 19475.

Delaware Valley Orienteering Association. 1999. French Creek Central Orienteering Map, including portions of French Creek State Park and Hopewell Village National Historic Site, DVOA, 14 Lake Drive, Spring City, PA 19475.

Droege, S., L. Monti, and D. Lantz. 1997. The Terrestrial Salamander Monitoring Program: Recommended Protocol for Running Cover Object Arrays. <http://www.im.nbs.gov/sally/sally4.html> [March 13, 2003].

Ernst, C. H. and R. W. Barbour. 1989. Snakes of eastern North America. George Mason University Press, Fairfax, VA. 282 pp.

Genoways, H. H. and Brenner, F. J. (Eds.). 1985. Species of special concern in Pennsylvania. Special Publication of the Carnegie Museum of Natural History, Number 11. Pittsburgh, PA. 430 pp.

Green, N. B. and T. K. Pauley. 1987. Amphibians and reptiles in West Virginia. University of Pittsburgh Press, Pittsburgh, PA. xi + 241 pp.

Heister, R. and E. B. Geer. 2001. State of our watersheds report: French Creek Watershed. Green Valleys Association, Pottstown, PA. <http://www.greenvalleys.org/sow/fc.html> [March 27, 2003].

Hulse, A. C., C. J. McCoy, and E. J. Censky. 2001. Amphibians and reptiles of Pennsylvania and the Northeast. Comstock Publishing Associates, Cornell University Press, Ithaca, NY. x + 419 pp.

Jung, R. 2002a. Northeast Amphibian Research and Monitoring Initiative, NE ARMI Projects, Stream Salamanders. <http://www.mp2-pwrc.usgs.gov/nearmi/projects/> [March 27, 2003].

Jung, R. 2002b. Northeast Amphibian Research and Monitoring Initiative, NE ARMI Projects, Vernal Pool Amphibians. <http://www.mp2-pwrc.usgs.gov/nearmi/projects/> [March 27, 2003].

Karr, J. R. 1997. Measuring biological integrity. Pages 483-485 in G. K. Meffe, and C. R. Carroll, editors. Principles of Consevation Biology. Second Edition. Sinauer Associates, Inc. Sunderland, MA. 729 pp.

Kaufmann, J. H. 1992. Habitat use by wood turtles in central Pennsylvania. J. Herpetology 26: 315-321.

Lowe, S., M. Browne, and S. Boudjelas. [no date]. 100 of the world's worst invasive alien species: a selection from the global invasive species database. Global Invasive Species Programme, University of Auckland, Auckland, NZ. < http://www.issg.org/booklet.pdf> [March 27, 2003].

McCoy, C. J. 1982. Amphibians and reptiles in Pennsylvania. Carnegie Museum of Natural History, Special Publication 6, Pittsburgh, PA. 91 pp.

Mertz, L. (Ed.). 1999. Protocols and Strategies for Monitoring North American Amphibians: Calling Surveys. North American Amphibian Monitoring Program, USGS [http://www.mp1-pwrc.usgs.gov/amphib/tools/proto-call.html].

Noss, R. F. 1997. Hierarchical indicators for monitoring changes in biodiversity. Pages 88-89 in G. K. Meffe, and C. R. Carroll, editors. Principles of Consevation Biology. Second Edition. Sinauer Associates, Inc. Sunderland, MA. 729 pp.

Palmer, W. A. and A. L. Braswell. 1995. Reptiles of North Carolina. University of North Carolina Press, Chapel Hill, NC. xiii + 412 pp.

Petranka, J. W. 1998. Salamanders of the United States and Canada. Smithsonian Institution Press, Washington, DC. xvi + 587 pp.

Pfingsten, R. A. and F. L. Downs. 1989. Salamanders of Ohio. Bulletin of the Ohio Biological Survey 7(2): xx + 315 pp.

Russell, E. W. B. 1987. Vegetation study Hopewell Furnace National Historic Site. Final Report 4-28211 DI-NPS-Hopewell Village. 94 pp.

Seigel, R. A., and J. S. Doody. 1996. Inventory and monitoring of amphibians and reptiles of the Gulf Islands National Seashore. Pp. 100-111 *In* T. R. Simons (Ed.). Coastal Park Inventory and Monitoring Handbook. Technical Report NPS/SERNCSU/NRTR-95/01.

Seigel, R. A., and T. Simons. 1995. Inventory and monitoring programs for endangered and indicator species of National Parks. Pp. 100-111 *In* T. R. Simons (Ed.). Coastal Park Inventory and Monitoring Handbook. Technical Report NPS/SERNCSU/NRTR-95/01.

Shaffer, L. L. 1991. Pennsylvania Amphibians and Reptiles. Pennsylvania Fish and Boat Commission, Harrisburg, PA. 161 pp.

Simons, T. R. 1995. Coastal Park Inventory and Monitoring Handbook. Technical Report NPS/SERNCSU/NRTR-95/01.

Somma, L. A., A. Foster, and P. Fuller. 2002. Nonindigenous aquatic species factsheet: *Trachemys scripta elegans*. U. S. Geological Survey . <http://nas.er.usgs.gov/queries/SpFactSheet.asp?speciesID=1261> [March 27, 2003}.

Tiebout III, H. M. 2003. An Inventory of the Herpetofauna of Valley Forge National Historical Park. Final Report. NPS Cooperative Agreement No. 4000-9-9016. 71 pp.

Tyning, T. F. 1990 A guide to amphibians and reptiles. Little, Brown and Company, New York, NY. xiv + 400 pp.

U. S. Fish and Wildlife Service. 2001. Guidelines for bog turtle surveys. <http://nyfo.fws.gov/es/btsurvey.pdf> [March 27, 2003].

Vanderwerff, W. D. 1994. The vascular flora of Hopewell Furnace National Historic Site. Unpublished report No. IT1010-HOFU. 42 pp.

Weir, L. 2001. North American Amphibian Monitoring Program. <http://www.mp2-pwrc.usgs.gov/naamp/> [March 27, 2003].

White, J. F., Jr., and A. W. White. 2002. Amphibians and Reptiles of Delmarva. Tidewater Publishers, Centreville, MD. xvi + 248 pp.

Wild Resource Conservation Fund. 1995. Endangered and threatened species of Pennsylvania. Harrisburg, PA. 80 pp.

Yahner, R. H., G. L. Storm, G. S. Keller, and R. W. Rohrbaugh, Jr. 1995. Progress Report: Inventorying and monitoring protocols of vertebrates in National Park areas of the eastern United States: Gettysburg National Military Park and Eisenhower National Historic Site. Cooperative Agreement 4000-9-8004. 113 pp.

Yahner, R. H., G. S. Keller, B. D. Ross, and R. W. Rohrbaugh, Jr. 1999. Inventorying and monitoring protocols of terrestrial vertebrates in National Parks of the eastern United States: Hopewell Furnace National Historic Site. Technical Report NPS/PHSO/NRTR-00/081. 194 pp.

Appendix - Glossary of Terms and Acronyms

ACS Anura Calling Survey

animal pen (habitat type) fenced area for holding sheep, other stock

ARMI Amphibian Research and Monitoring Initiative, USGS

building/grounds (habitat type) historical structures, residences, park buildings, and associated grounds

corn field (habitat type) cultivated corn fields

encounter detection of an animal during a survey. Because animals were not individually marked, an encounter is not the same as an individual animal (i.e., multiple detections of the same animal at different times were recorded as multiple encounters).

French Creek (habitat type) within 1 m of French Creek

GHC General Herpetological Collecting

GPS global positioning system

habitat general description of landscape features typical of where a species occurs; not the same as habitat type

habitat type one of 14 categories of habitat used in the inventory, includes habitats and structures that are natural (e.g., lowland forest) and anthropogenic (e.g., buildings)

hay field (habitat type) cultivated hayfields, mowed regularly

HDI = Habitat Diversity Index = $H' = -\sum Log_{10}(p_i)*(p_i)$

> where p_i = the proportion of total sightings for a given species that occurred in habitat type i

HOFU Hopewell Furnace National Historic Site

lowland forest (habitat type) deciduous forest in floodplain of French Creek or of lower Baptism Creek, level terrain with standing water or subject to seasonal flooding

mixed (habitat type) mixture of two or more habitat types

NAAMP North American Amphibian Monitoring Program, USGS

NPS National Park Service

observation any datum recorded is considered an observation (e.g., SVL for a particular salamander)

open wetland (habitat type) wetlands with little or no canopy, may be seasonally wet only

pasture (habitat type) grassy fields for grazing of domestic stock

PS Project Statement from a VAFO resource management plan

PSU Pennsylvania State University

RMP resource management plan

rock field (habitat type) areas of large rocks or boulders, with or without forest canopy

run (habitat type) within 1 m of small streams, includes all runs, Baptism Creek north of Hopewell Road, all tributaries to Baptism Creek, all tributaries to French Creek

survey all surveying done on a given date using the same method was considered a single survey

SVL snout-vent length

TSMP Terrestrial Salamander Monitoring Program, USGS

upland forest (habitat type) deciduous forest not subject to flooding, does not have standing water

USGS United States Geological Survey

UTM universal transverse mercator map projection for GIS

vernal pool (habitat type) any of several vernal pools located in the southern floodplain of French Creek between Hopewell Lake and Hopewell

WCU West Chester University, West Chester, PA

weedy field (habitat type) uncultivated fields, usually the power line right-of-way

WOCs Wildlife Observation Cards, reported in Yahner et al. (1999)